Monk's Notre Dame

"As a student, administrator, faculty member, priest-in-residence, and more, Fr. Malloy has seen our university from virtually every perspective. This book gives us all the opportunity to learn from and enjoy Notre Dame as seen through the eyes of my predecessor as president, fellow Holy Cross priest, and friend, Monk Malloy. I recommend it for anyone who loves Notre Dame or wants to better know this special place."

—*Rev. John I. Jenkins, C.S.C., president, University of Notre Dame*

"With humility, humor, and keen insight, in *Monk's Notre Dame* Fr. Malloy chronicles the people, places, sights, and sounds that make up this special place. In these pages, he emerges as Notre Dame's master tour guide and bard."

—*Patricia A. O'Hara, professor emerita of law, University of Notre Dame*

"Yet another remarkable work from a prolific writer, mentor, and educator, *Monk's Notre Dame* is a fast-paced, easy-to-digest, and expansive series of vignettes on all aspects of life at Notre Dame. Undoubtedly, this extraordinary book will become a must-read for the Notre Dame aficionado or casual fan."

—*Lou Nanni, vice president of university relations, University of Notre Dame*

"For those who know Notre Dame (and even those who don't!), *Monk's Notre Dame* is sure to delight. This heartwarming 'narrative of the institution' is full of stories and anecdotes that bring to life the essence of Notre Dame told from the perspective of one of her most loyal sons. I will surely recommend it to all the alumni of Notre Dame."

—*Dolly Duffy, executive director, University of Notre Dame Alumni Association*

"The stories and essays that compose *Monk's Notre Dame* speak to the singularity of this university as a place full of rich traditions, strong faith, and authentic community. With warmth and humility, Fr. Malloy gives us the sort of insights that come only with a lifetime spent serving Our Lady's university."

—*Shannon Cullinan, executive vice president, University of Notre Dame*

"Over the course of a half-century, few have had the opportunity to observe Notre Dame from as many perspectives (student, student-athlete, dorm staff, professor, administrator, university president) as Fr. Monk Malloy. In *Monk's Notre Dame*, he shares a collection of colorful anecdotes, a historical glimpse of the people, places, and events defining the life of the university during his tenure. My unexpected delight was how many of his reflections unearthed long-forgotten personal recollections and reminded me of the unique nature of each Notre Dame experience."

—*Missy Conboy, senior deputy director of athletics, University of Notre Dame*

"After more than forty years as student, professor, and top administrator at the University of Notre Dame, Fr. Edward 'Monk' Malloy reminisces about the institution he has served and loved. Anecdotes abound of idiosyncratic professors, residence hall pranks, Holy Week liturgies, peculiarities of campus buildings, athletic victories and defeats, and insights into the author's own personality through it all."

—*Rev. Thomas E. Blantz, C.S.C., author of*
The University of Notre Dame: A History

MONK'S

NOTRE DAME

MONK'S

NOTRE DAME

REVEREND EDWARD A. MALLOY, C.S.C.

University of Notre Dame Press

Notre Dame, Indiana

Illustrations copyright © 2005 by Robert F. Ringel

Paperback edition published in 2022

Library of Congress Cataloging-inPublication Data

Malloy, Edward A.
Monk's Notre Dame / Edward A. Malloy.
p. cm.
ISBN: 978-0-268-03497-9 (hardback)
ISBN: 978-0-268-20245-3 (paperback)
1. University of Notre Dame—Anecdotes.   2. Malloy, Edward A.   I. Title.
LD4112.9.M35   2005
378.772'89—dc22
2005019768

Contents

MEMORABLE INDIVIDUALS

OF THIS AND THAT

Introduction

Every higher educational community is constantly renewing itself with new people and new sets of experiences. However, in order to pass the traditions and the lore on to the next generation, the carriers of the ethos of the place introduce those newly arrived into the larger narrative of the institution. As someone has remarked, Notre Dame is a carried book. And as a result, it is of necessity a prime locus for storytelling. For example, when new students move into a dormitory, the upperclassmen indoctrinate them from the start by telling them stories about the distinctive traditions of the residence hall, or exploits that they and their peers engaged in during the previous year, or the personality traits and character of the rector of the dorm.

The same thing happens when new faculty join an academic department or college. Their peers make them feel comfortable and establish the human dimensions of the place by telling stories about favorite or problematic classes of students, or grumpy colleagues, or penny-pinching deans, or special moments when colleagues have bonded together to support one another at a time of death or difficulty.

As Notre Dame has become more complex and larger in scale, administrators have made a conscious effort to develop introductory workshops and retreats to speed up the process by which new faculty or staff might feel part of the institution. For example, in recent years the university administration has sponsored a two-day retreat for new faculty and their spouses and families. They learn from respected teachers, hear rectors describe the importance of the residential tradition, or listen to the president or provost as he encourages their academic productivity and calms their fears about standards that will prevail at time of promotion.

There is no occasion in which storytelling at Notre Dame is more rampant than during Alumni Reunion Weekend. On that occasion each summer, graduates return to the university in five-year increments. They come back to look back, to regain a sense of their common heritage while reacquainting themselves with the geography of the campus

1

as well as its current activities. Even when returning graduates did not know each other when they were students, they quickly discover that they share a memorable history. When someone asks, "Do you remember the time . . . ?" others can fill in the blanks, either from firsthand experience or from tales told to them by their peers through the years. Not only do reunion weekends foster class identity, but they also allow the alumni/ae to find a common intergenerational identity as they relate the stories and sing the songs and wear the colors. Even those who have not returned to the campus for decades are invariably moved by simply being on sacred ground.

The origin of this collection of stories and essays was my notion that I had a responsibility to share with others the many tales passed on to me. Some of these experiences were humorous, some poignant, and others revelatory about the kind of institution that we have become. As a member of the founding religious community, I also knew stories about community members who had played special roles in the life of the institution—stories that might not be well known to others.

I then began not only to recover stories out of my own memory bank but also to solicit contributions from others. Having begun the process of reflection about the distinctive features of the Notre Dame experience, I also considered the general dimensions of the life of the institution that might be worthy of an essay format. The Notre Dame campus is a defined space, but its internal life is vibrant and ever changing. I looked for parallels between one time in our history and another. As someone who lives on the campus 24-7, as they say, I was aware of the rhythms of the calendar and academic years in a way that some others might not be. I also have been privileged to have had a number of special opportunities as university president (as well as teacher, pastor, and dorm resident) that prompted me to think about aspects of a common life with which others might empathize.

My personal library of Notre Dame–related books fills almost three long shelves. Some of the volumes have to do with Notre Dame athletics, but there is a growing literature that covers different aspects of Notre Dame's history, treats elements of our distinctiveness as a Catholic university, or relates to various organizations or traditions, or tries to capture some of the vitality of an academic unit. This book is intended to complement those other works. Indeed, my joy and interest in reading other Notre Dame–related volumes has motivated me to make my own contribution to this growing literature.

In a special way I want to thank Dick Conklin for his assistance in organizing the material and in helping to prepare it for publication, as well as Bob Ringel for his illustrations. Both are Notre Dame retirees, in public relations and campus architecture, respectively, who brought their own institutional memories to the task. Special mention goes also to the staff of the Notre Dame Press, whose manuscript tweaks ensured a better book.

I hope that the work as a whole can strike some common chord, not only in the experience of those who have studied, taught, or worked at the university but also for the legion of people interested in Notre Dame and all that makes it special. In the end, this book was a labor of love, and I hope my readers can share my pleasure in, once again, telling the stories of a place dear to us all.

Reverend Edward A. (Monk) Malloy, C. S.C.
President Emeritus, University of Notre Dame

Flunk-Out or President?

At Archbishop John Carroll High School in Washington, D.C., I received a wonderful education from the Augustinian priests and brothers. Despite the fact that I was heavily involved in athletics and other extracurricular activities, I was always a good student and took my academic responsibilities seriously. I graduated third in my class and was heavily recruited as a scholarship athlete in basketball by many colleges, at least partially because of my strong academic credentials.

One of my teachers at Carroll was an Augustinian priest who, in a physics course at the time after Sputnik had succeeded in sending the Soviet Union first into space, convinced us that if we possessed natural academic gifts, we had almost a moral obligation to study either science or engineering in college. In retrospect this seems a totally inappropriate way to pick a major. But I decided, on the basis of this exhortation, to study engineering at Notre Dame. Thus, as the first semester of my freshman year proceeded, I was listed as a chemical engineering student, even though I didn't have the slightest idea what a chemical engineer did. However, the real problem began when I did not like my math teacher and toward the end of the semester stopped going to class. I also had progressively greater difficulty in my engineering drawing class. Meanwhile, I was reading a lot of novels on the side.

In those days, the fall semester at Notre Dame was not completed until after the Christmas break. Then on one fateful day in January I received my grades for the first semester. I discovered that I had flunked both math and engineering drawing and was .01 points from flunking out of the university entirely. My math grade reflected both a lack of interest and a lack of motivation. In my final exam in engineering drawing I thought I had gotten one hundred, but I ended up with a zero, which indicated that I was far from understanding the basic principles of the class. The same day that I got my grades, I went to downtown South Bend and watched the hit movie of the day, *A Summer Place*, twice in a row while I sat off in a corner of the theater crying and feeling sorry for myself.

Since according to the NCAA rules of the day, freshmen were ineligible to play in the second semester of the first year anyway, my dismal academic situation didn't affect my eligibility as a practice participant with the basketball team. I soon got sound advice from the Academic Counseling Office and, after taking a battery of tests, determined that I should major either in English or history. I chose English, and my academic fortunes took a quick turn for the better. At the end of the second semester of my first year I was off probation, and in subsequent years ably pursued an English major in the College of Arts and Letters.

While this experience was traumatic at the time, I look back with full appreciation for how it redirected my life in a way that made me much happier and academically successful. I have great respect for engineering as a field, but I simply was not cut out for it. With my background, temperament, and talent, I was much better qualified to study one of the humanities. After completing my bachelor's degree in English, I went on to master's degrees in English and theology and my Ph.D. in Christian Ethics. Ironically, when I took my GRE exams to qualify for the Ph.D. program at Vanderbilt, I tested in the 97th percentile in math, even though I had had no more math classes since my makeup course during the second semester of my first year at Notre Dame.

My rocky start in college has given me great sympathy for undergraduate students who have done well in high school and are now faced with making the transition to college. Some of them choose majors for which they are ill-suited because of pressure from their parents, while others have to learn a new set of study skills and discipline in order to succeed in college. Still others have unsettling setbacks that lower their motivation, and they need time to recover. Whatever the reason, I like to tell undergraduates who have difficulties in their first year that there is still hope for them. I remind them that I had the good fortune to become the president of the school where I almost flunked out.

IN THE HALLS

Moving In

From the time that prospective undergraduates receive their letters of admission until the week of First-Year Orientation, the new students and their parents are inundated with information from the Admissions Office, the Financial Aid Office, the Registrar, the First Year of Studies, and the Alumni Association. Everyone wants these students to get off to an excellent start. Some of the young people first visited Notre Dame with their parents when they were babes-in-arms, others attended one of the summer camps, and still others stayed in the Alumni Family Hall, but there are many who never set foot on campus until they arrive for orientation.

The goal of the orientation process is to make the students feel at home as quickly as possible and to provide them with information useful in the long run. Some parts of the orientation activities are designed primarily for the parents, while others are geared to the students. The newcomers can quickly go into sensory overload as they listen to rectors and hall staff, counselors in the First Year of Studies, representatives of the university administration, directors of various student activities, and athletic coaches. Indeed, I often receive appreciative letters from parents after they return home indicating how comfortable they felt leaving their pride and joy, their son or daughter, behind on campus. Many of their questions were answered during First-Year Orientation.

Perhaps the most critical component of the orientation process involves moving into the residence halls. My impression is that on many campuses this is left to the initiative of the families, with some advice from the rector of the dorm and from some of the staff. But at Notre Dame, the hall staffs and many upperclass volunteers come days ahead of time to prepare the way—to ensure that all the time slots are covered, that all receive assistance in moving their belongings into the dorm, and that there are no glitches in the process. Many of the dorm volunteers wear a distinctive T-shirt that celebrates the hall's identity and distinguishes them from the mass of other students.

Outside of the dorms, there are temporary university workers, usually semi-retired men and women in yellow jackets, who make sure that the parking places adjacent to the dorms are divvied up properly and that no one overstays his time. They also serve as security for the various items left in cars and on the lawns while the families are taking one load after another inside.

In some of the older residence halls, where the unfurnished rooms can seem quite barren and unattractive, it is important to reassure the parents that all of the rooms will eventually look like home when they have been furnished and decorated. I have often heard parents, who are already experiencing high levels of separation anxiety, saying things like, "You expect my son (or daughter) to live in this slum?" This impression is exacerbated by the fact that most of the first-year students have at least one, and often two or three, roommates. Once the several roommates all have their stuff lying out in the room, some hard decisions have to be made. If there are four televisions or four CD players or three or four of anything, they agree to share a limited number of options. This compromise frees up some space and creates the climate of give-and-take that will be necessary in the coming year.

For many years in some of these same venerable dorms, it was customary to build lofts for layered sleeping arrangements as well as shelving so as to maximize the use of vertical space. However, few of the parents had the do-it-yourself skills to construct a safe and attractive loft on the spot. One of my brothers-in-law, John Long, whose three daughters eventually graduated from Notre Dame, became famous in his time for not only happily building the lofts for his daughters and their roommates but also making himself available to others who were less handy. The word would go down the corridor that at least one parent was able to solve the nettlesome problem of loft building. John never took any money for his yeoman service.

One time when I was an assistant rector in Sorin Hall, I was showing the family of a first- year student the basement-level room that their son would occupy. They were one of the late arrivals, and there was only one bed left in the double room. I was sure that one of the other new arrivals had appropriated the other bed. I assured the family that they would have a bed for their son in no time at all, and we borrowed an upperclassman's, which gave us a few days to replace it.

The oddest experience that I can recall was the father of a student who was in a special program in Europe and could not get to the campus in time for orientation. The father simply took his place, moved into the dorm with his son's roommates-to-be, went to all the orientation sessions as if he were a freshman, and even attended the first few days of classes and took notes. I am sure that the father was simply trying to get his son off to a good start, but one can imagine the reaction of the young man's roommates and the other first-year students when they saw someone their own father's age trekking around with them to all the events.

In the last analysis, the residential tradition is one of the great and distinctive strengths of Notre Dame as a university. And from my experience and the testimony of others, the vast majority of new students and families get off to a good start in the dorms. The hard work and enthusiasm of the hall staffs and the volunteers are a big part of making this happen from year to year. Transitions are never easy, and some students need more time than others to get acclimated. But the residence halls really do become one's home away from home during the four years at Notre Dame. A colleague once told me of his freshman nephew who concluded Thanksgiving with his family by saying, "Well, I have to go home now." He was referring to a place where he had spent only two months.

Hall Mascots

As Notre Dame has evolved as an undergraduate institution, it has tried to preserve the distinctiveness of the residential tradition. There are currently twenty-seven male and female residence halls (fourteen male and thirteen female), and each of these dorms has its own culture and traditions. The older dorms such as Sorin, St. Edward's, Cavanaugh, and Badin lack some of the comforts of the newer ones, such as air conditioning, large study areas, and well-designed social spaces, but they have a longer history and more variety in the types and shapes of living accommodations. Sorin, Walsh, and Badin have porches, which are pleasant places to watch the world go by. Keenan, Stanford, Howard, and Dillon are right next to dining halls. Pangborn is adjacent to the Rock, or Rockne Memorial. Siegfried and Knott are close to the Hesburgh Library. Keough, O'Neill Family, McGlinn, and Welsh Family are closest to the bookstore.

Farley celebrates Pop Farley Week each year to honor a beloved priest, Reverend John F. Farley, C.S.C. Dillon holds a pep rally on the first home football weekend. Carroll, with an expansive lawn, has the advantage of having the smallest number of students as it tries to nurture a sense of community each year. The Fisher Regatta energizes St. Mary's Lake each spring with a competition among dorms for the speediest or most intriguing watercraft.

One thing that each of the dorms has in common is a hall mascot. These mascots can be divided into three general categories. The first are animals: the Badin Bullfrogs, Howard Ducks, Lewis Chickens, Pangborn Phoxes, Pasquerilla West Purple Weasels, Alumni Hall Dawgs, Keough Kangaroos, Sorin Screaming Otters, Carroll Vermin. The Carroll mascot's name is a not-so-subtle reference to the age of the dorm and the suspicion that more critters than men reside therein. One might call the second group images of aggressive action: the Dillon Big Red, Fisher Green Wave, Keenan Knights, Knott Juggernauts, O'Neill Angry Mob,

Siegfried Ramblers, Cavanaugh Chaos, Pasquerilla East Pyros, Walsh's Wild Women, Welsh Family Whirlwinds. These names or mascots seem best suited for athletic interhall competition rather than for social interchange.

The third category might be described as idiosyncractic nicknames sometimes flowing out of the hall name or its history or some imaginative connection: the Breen-Phillips Babes, Farley's Finest, Lyons Lions (also an animal reference), Morrissey the Manor, Men of St. Edward's, Zahm's Zombies (also aggressive), Stanford's Griffins. Stanford used to be known as the Studs, which seemed a bit too suggestive, so the name was changed to the Griffins in honor of Father Bob Griffin, C.S.C., who lived in the hall for many years and for a period of time served as rector. From my experience I would say that some of the halls take their mascots more seriously than others, and some of the nicknames are more in-your-face than others.

A sampling of some of the signs put up during Freshman Orientation Week further reveals the peculiar nicknames and self-image of many of the dorms. Lyons Hall announces its presence with the encouragement, "Let Us Hear You Roar." Badin Hall proclaims, "Quality, not Quantity," which refers to the relatively small size of the dorm. Zahm Hall boasts a number of signs, including "Zahm—The Best Six Years of Your Life," "Zahm—You'll Love All Seven Years," and "On the Eighth Day, Zahm." Breen-Phillips has two signs: "I Got U Babe" and "BP=Best Place." Pasquerilla West declares that "The West Is the Best," while Pasquerilla East proclaims, "Welcome to the Firehouse," which refers to the Pyros nickname. Carroll Hall, which is somewhat off the beaten path, calls itself "Your Home Away from Home . . . and Campus." Finally, Sorin Hall, where I live, is like being in neutral Switzerland, since the students learn quickly that it is the university's oldest residence and has its own special sense of tradition and pride. As a result, the dorm neither has signs nor sends its new students around the campus during Orientation Week to sing its praises. Sorinites would consider such behavior beneath them.

With the passage of time, many things have changed about dorm life at Notre Dame. The formal rules are much less strict than they once were, and the spirit of a particular dorm is often influenced heavily for better or for worse by a longtime rector. Also, the prior experience of residents in family homes and in secondary schools can affect the satisfaction level they have with their collegiate living environment.

Nevertheless, all things being equal, the dorm residents at Notre Dame take great pride in their living place and carry away indelible experiences of friendship, of worship and of fellowship from the sharing that marks these diverse but spirit-filled residence halls.

The Rector and the Casket

One of the distinctive facets of the residence hall heritage here at Notre Dame is the way in which the various traditions of a particular hall are created, reinforced, then flourish for awhile, and either continue or disappear because of lack of interest or because it is time for a change. One such tradition is Alumni Hall Week. Alumni Hall, which was built in the 1930s, has declared itself the "Center of the Universe." No matter what anyone thinks of this self-designation, this dormitory has been a vital part of Notre Dame for some seventy years.

The current rector of Alumni Hall, Father George Rozum, C.S.C., now reigns as the dean among university rectors. He is much beloved by the students who have lived in his dorm. George suffers from a wide variety of allergies and, as a result, has a reputation for being somewhat fastidious. He is not inclined toward practical jokes, excessive revelry, or

a prominent public posture. Nevertheless, once the tradition of Alumni Hall Week developed, Father George began to play a central role.

The Alumni Hall Week began as an excuse in the dreary times of second semester for an all-hall party. It was fashioned in imitation of a traditional Irish wake, complete with a rented, regular wooden casket. The hall would be decorated, and the residents and their dates would be getting into the spirit of the occasion. Then, at a climactic moment, much to the surprise of the first-year students, a closed coffin would be carried through the corridors, and down to the large lounge in the basement. Then, to much fanfare, the lid of the casket would be taken off and up would spring Father George, dressed in a white evening coat with a green cummerbund and a green tie, who would proceed to address the assembled guests. Year after year, the same startling appearance would be repeated, and it became a long-expected part of the wake for veterans and a recurring surprise for the uninitiated.

Then one year, just as the closed casket was being carried through the dorm, the fire alarm went off in Alumni Hall. When the Notre Dame Fire Department arrived, they made their way along the corridor to where the casket was being held aloft. The fire chief called out, "Who's the rector here?" Much to their astonishment, the coffin opened and Father George sat up and timidly proclaimed, "I am." Once they had gotten over their shock, the firemen cleared the hall until it was determined that there was no further risk. As far as I know, upon returning to their station house, the fire chief and his mates took it all in stride. They had always wondered about those crazy rectors, anyway.

Hot and Cold

One way of describing the campus facilities is to distinguish those that have air conditioning from those that do not. Generally, the classroom and administrative buildings as well as the laboratories and other workspaces are tied into the campus heating and cooling grid. Cool air is provided in the summer and hot air in the winter. When the power plant is functioning smoothly, there are few, if any, complaints about the system.

The newer residence halls are also tied into the heating and cooling system and have controlled environments comparable to the academic offices. But the core group of older halls are no different in their temperature controls than when they were first constructed. Thus, the dorms in the Main Quad, in the North Quad, and Sorin, Walsh, and Carroll Halls all lack air conditioning. (There are a few exceptions, such as the Keenan-Stanford chapel, which has often, because of its size, served as a backup worship space for large Masses.)

During the regular school year, there are only a couple of weeks when the rooms and chapels might be really uncomfortable when it comes to heat and humidity. Most students buy fans and may even keep their room doors open for air circulation on particularly hot days and evenings. But beyond that, students wear as little clothing as possible and simply tough it out.

When it comes to the staff rooms, usually there are window air conditioners that make the older dorms tolerable for the rectors, assistant rectors, and in-residence people. But even then, some of us prefer natural cooling, aided by an overhead rotating fan, like those in the old British empire movies set in India. That is the case with my own living space in Sorin Hall. I keep the windows open on hot, humid days, have my two fans moving at a moderate pace, and otherwise relish a temperature pattern that I personally prefer.

The real problem in the older dorms comes in the summertime, when the regular students aren't around and other groups inhabit the dorms for various programs. This is especially problematic for whichever dorms are designated as halls for returning alumni and their families. Many come with younger children who may be accustomed to air conditioning. Parents tell their offspring to make the best of it and enjoy all of the campus recreational facilities and opportunities. Indeed, families can swim in the pools or in the lake, ride bicycles, go to special events, and otherwise treat the campus like summer camp.

I cannot imagine what it must have been like years ago when there was no central heating in the living spaces on campus. On the very bleakest days of January or February, it must have been a challenge indeed. That partly explains why students and staff took a bath once a week at most and slept in heavy covers with a minimum number of trips out of bed. I am sure that the priests and brothers and lay people who founded Notre Dame, if they came back today, would be surprised at all of the comforts and conveniences that we enjoy. Perhaps none would strike them more dramatically than our ability to control the temperature in our living and working spaces throughout the course of the year.

Mass in the Halls

When Father, later Cardinal, John O'Hara, C.S.C., was the head of what we now call Campus Ministry, he was a great advocate of the regular reception of the Holy Eucharist. This was in the wake of Pope Pius X and his encouragement of frequent Eucharistic participation. Today we take it for granted that when people attend the Eucharist, either on Sunday or during the week, they will receive Communion. But in the early part of the twentieth century and before, because of a great emphasis on human sinfulness as well as on an individual's own unworthiness, many people who went to Mass would not receive Communion. However, from Father O'Hara's time on, Notre Dame has been a Eucharist-centered campus. Each of the dormitories has its own chapel, and it was expected that on weekdays Mass would be held every morning in these chapels. One way of encouraging students to participate in my own time was "morning check," in which each student in the dorm was expected to show up, properly dressed, at a certain time to sign in next to the chapel two or three times per week. No one formally insisted that the students had to go to Mass, but it was heavily promoted.

In my era, in the 1960s, students went to Sunday Mass in Sacred Heart Church. But as the size of the student body grew and the number of dormitories increased, students typically attended Sunday liturgies in their own dorms. This was especially the case after the reforms of Vatican II. The dorm Masses, characterized by music that most students found attractive and even inspiring, became more informal and more dependent upon the participation of students in various liturgical roles.

From the late 1960s on, the typical Notre Dame student worshiped on the weekend in his or her dorm, and some smaller percentage would also participate in the weekday Masses when they were available. As the number of Masses proliferated, so did the expectation that there would be a sufficient number of clergy available to guarantee a celebrant for each liturgy on campus. These dorm Masses became over time a characteristic mode of Notre Dame residential life. I know of no other campus in the country where the Eucharist is so available, so regularly participated in, and so influential in developing the lifetime habits of the participants. In the years since I have been president, I have attempted to go to as many dormitories for Sunday Mass as possible during the course of the school year. I have also responded to invitations to worship with the MBA students, the graduate students, different undergraduate classes, and other subgroups in the Notre Dame community.

The tone at Notre Dame is set liturgically by the large Mass in the basketball arena at the time of Freshmen Orientation, as well as the more recent tradition of a campus-wide, beginning-of-the-school-year Mass on Tuesday during the first week of classes. This campus-wide Mass also takes place in the basketball arena and is followed by a picnic and a fireworks display. It is heavily attended, including by faculty and staff and their families, and informs the perception of the kind of community we are to those whom we are newly welcoming into our ranks.

It is taken for granted in each of our dormitories, including in Fischer and O'Hara-Grace, which are populated exclusively by professional and graduate students, that there will be a chapel, a liturgical committee, a music group, and a regular schedule of Masses and other liturgical opportunities. These dorm chapels vary in size and elaborateness. Alumni Hall's chapel, for example, is beautifully appointed and even has its own endowment. Some chapels are more traditional, with pews and kneelers, and others are more contemporary, with either movable chairs or a tendency for the congregation to sit on the floor.

One of the challenges for the rector of each dorm is to provide high-quality music from year to year. Since the music ministers are volunteers and their talent can vary from one academic year to another, the final product sometimes is better and more warmly received than at other times. In some dorms, one student is predominantly responsible for organizing the music and inviting musicians and singers. At this time in Notre Dame's history, the music at Masses tends to be much more biblical and theologically focused than it was in the immediate wake of Vatican II. At that time, in the pause after Communion, one often heard songs from popular culture that were only marginally religious in content or meaning.

One of the most interesting changes that has happened through the years comes at the singing of the Lord's Prayer as well as at the exchange of peace. Now it is taken for granted that the congregation will hold hands during the singing of the Lord's Prayer in both the male and female dorms. Earlier, it was more likely to happen only in the women's dorms. Moreover, a hug at the exchange of peace is more common today in both men's and women's dorms, where previously in the men's dorms, a handshake was the norm.

Dorm liturgies tend to be informal in dress. When the weather is hot, the students often appear in shorts and a T-shirt with or without shoes. Since it is basically a peer culture, no one thinks twice about how one is dressed. The students are more intent upon enjoying each other's company. In some of the women's dorms they wear amusing animal slippers, which look like bears or muskrats or rabbits. It can be a little disconcerting to look down and wonder whether one is at a menagerie or a zoo.

Campus Ministry provides instruction in the fall for all who exercise liturgical ministries in the dorms and in the Basilica. This ensures that the Scripture readings are done with fitting dignity and that Communion is distributed properly. There is no absence of piety among the students. Despite the informality of some aspects of the liturgy, these are genuine situations of worship in which to praise the Living God.

From my experience and the feedback I receive from the students, generally the quality of the preaching is quite good. Because of the uniformity of the congregation, the priest can easily draw upon a common fund of experience and interests. Students are always preoccupied by the fragility of relationships, by the concern to make the world a better place, by the stresses and strains of a competitive academic environment, and by the complicated decisions about what they want to do after graduation. It is often during the prayer of the faithful that one learns about particular concerns of individual students. There are prayers about a family member who has recently died, or about a parent or sibling who is sick, or about a peer from high school who committed suicide or died in an auto accident. There are prayers not only in response to international issues or social concerns but also in joy at the birth of a new child in the family.

One of the big challenges for our graduates is to find worship settings that are comparable once they move away from the Notre Dame environment. Part of this search may simply be an effort to preserve the college years forever, but it also has to do with the aging of the clergy, the greater difficulty in finding liturgical settings that are attractive and comfortable, and the hectic life that so many of our graduates lead when they begin their next level of education or their professional careers. For most of our students, the days of worshiping out of guilt are gone. Now, as young adults, they need to make decisions about how their participation in the Catholic Church will respond to a deep hunger for the presence of the Living God and for a supportive community that can help them through the challenges of everyday life. From my experience, the community of faith, worship, and service is alive and well here at Notre Dame. May we always be such a vibrant university.

Sleep Sound

One of the great challenges for staff people living in the dormitories is how to deal with the outbreak of noise, which is an inevitable part of student life. Some rooms in dorms are strategically located so that the disruptive impact of noise is limited. Other rooms are, unfortunately, located on main corridors or are adjacent to outdoor student gathering places. As a general principle, the newer dorms' rooms for rectors, assistant rectors, priests and brothers, sisters, and lay people in residence are better insulated than in the older dorms. But a significant variable is what group of students happens to live next to the staff person's room in a given year, either on the same floor or on an adjacent floor.

In my early years in Sorin Hall, when I lived on the second floor at the point of conjunction of two long hallways, I found that it was difficult to separate my inner sanctum from the noises in the corridor and in nearby rooms. Fortunately, I tended to go to bed somewhere between two and three o'clock in the morning, and I outlasted the students themselves. The biggest challenge was on Friday and Saturday nights, when student fun and frivolity continue into the wee hours of the morning.

When I became a vice president, I decided to try and get my rooms better sound-proofed. But then I learned about another tactic, which I have employed ever since. I purchased from a catalog company a device called Sleep Sound, which is a small motor that generates continuous white noise. It absorbs extraneous noises to a degree that makes it easier for me to relax and go to sleep. It is not foolproof, since noise sufficiently loud still penetrates my consciousness, but it is a big step forward.

Even in the summer, when the students are not around, I use my Sleep Sound device because it induces a spirit of relaxation prior to sleep. I was introduced to this machine by a former rector who swore by it and who had also acquainted other rectors and some students with it. There are versions that can imitate the sounds of waves breaking on the shore or of birds chirping in the woods, but I have become accustomed to a simple mechanical sound like the hum of an electrical motor. In recent years, when I have been an administrator and needed to go to bed earlier and get up earlier as well as to look semi-refreshed as I began the workday, my Sleep Sound machine has become an integral part of my survival as a resident in a student dorm.

Annual Pigsty Award

Some percentage of the student body, especially in a male dorm, once they are away from their family's supervising eyes, revert to almost a pre-civilized standard of cleanliness and orderliness. They fail to make the connection between dirt and grime and sickness. They always know that if their parents come to visit for the weekend, they can do a quick cleanup and avoid too much censure. Of course, not all male students take this path in college, but enough of them do so that when I was assistant rector in Sorin Hall, I used to give the annual Pigsty Award to the room that best exemplified poor standards of cleanliness and attractiveness.

I never had any defined criteria for making the award, other than a quick judgment at the end of the school year about the combination of leftover pizza, fast-food hamburger wrappers, smashed crackers, uneaten bread, half-eaten candy bars, moldy popcorn, empty soft-drink and beer bottles, and a messy array of discarded socks, dirty underwear, old clothes, and trash. One sure way of narrowing down the list of potential winners was the foul odor test. If the stink was strong enough, it was a sure sign that I had a contender. In the end, the decision was relatively easy. Outside of the hall no announcement was made, and of course the parents never found out. I am confident that the same male students who won the Pigsty Award during their days at Sorin Hall turned out to be quite respectable husbands and fathers who regularly ordered their children to clean up their rooms.

Bat Boy

It took place at move-in time during Orientation Week. I was standing on Sorin Hall's porch with the father of one of the incoming freshmen while the newly arrived students were meeting their roommates and getting settled. All of a sudden, some students came rushing out onto the porch to report that one of the new freshmen had been bitten by a bat.

Bats sometimes appear in the hall when the students move in because they have nested in the attic undisturbed over the course of the

summer. Twice I have awakened in my room to find bats after I had left the door open because of the heat or to make myself available to those who were moving in. While most people would agree that bats serve a useful purpose in nature by eating mosquitoes and other insects, not too many people enjoy having them share their bedrooms. In any case, a bat had been flying around the corridor and somehow made its way into a freshman triple. The students in the room and some of their confreres decided to spread out a sheet to catch the bat, which worked. But then a young man tried to grab it by its tail. As it turned out, the father and mother of the bitten student were physicians and not easily daunted. The father himself had also lived for a year in Sorin Hall when he was an undergraduate. Rather than shout and scream or threaten to sue the university, the father simply proposed to kill the bat and bring it to the Indiana State Public Health Office for an autopsy to determine whether it was rabid. His son had to get rabies shots for a couple of weeks until the Public Health Office reported that the bat indeed was not rabid. The most lasting effect of the incident was that this new student went through his whole first year in college with the nickname "Bat Boy."

Two Cases of Grand Larceny

An ever astute rector was patrolling his dorm in the wee hours on a weekend morning. He observed two students attempting to steal candy from one of the second-floor vending machines. They were duly confronted, and their case was eventually passed on to the hall's judiciary board. As punishment, the two students were told to purchase enough M&Ms and Snickers bars for each of the residents of the dorm. The candy was then to be distributed outside of the rector's room during a ninety-minute period. If any candy remained unclaimed at the end, it was to be donated to a charity designated by the judiciary board. Thus, sweet justice was done.

In the days after Holy Cross Hall had ceased to be a seminary of the Holy Cross religious community, it functioned for many years as a male student residence hall. The nickname of the hall was "The Hogs," and its denizens constructed a magnificent pink pig for a mascot—a sturdy sheet of plywood about ten feet long and five feet high mounted on a wheeled platform. It was usually kept in the lobby of Holy Cross Hall so that it would be available when the residents wanted to take it to sporting events. One night, several residents of a rival hall from another end of the campus were in the Holy Cross lobby for a party. When no one was around, they tore the wooden pig off its base and took off with it toward the Carroll Hall side of the lake. They then pitched it over the golf course fence. Later that night, some of them went back and retrieved the pig and put it in their dormitory room, where it remained for about two weeks. Meanwhile, they kept calling Holy Cross residents to taunt them about the missing pig. Finally, someone got wind of where the kidnapped pig was being kept. In a panic, the abductors again tossed it over the fence of the golf course, called the president of Holy Cross, and told him where it could be found. The residents of Holy Cross collected their missing mascot. This incident is proof that thieves cannot keep their mouths shut.

A Savvy Rector

It was in the early 1980s, a Saturday night after a home football game in one of the older quads on campus. The experienced rector, who usually went to bed around midnight, observed a rope ladder descending right in front of his ground-floor bedroom window. Soon, three attractive young women went up the ladder. The rector, old pro that he was, waited until they were safely ensconced in the student room above his own, then ascended to the third floor and knocked on the students' door. The freshmen were very chagrined that they had been caught. It turned out that the young ladies were sisters and friends of the residents and in need of a place to spend the night. When asked why they thought they could pull off the rope trick, the students said, in all innocence, "We thought that the rector went home to sleep and only worked in the dormitory from 8 a.m. to 5 p.m." Unimpressed, the rector responded by levying a fine but did not discipline them for breaking parietals.

Winning the Heart of a Rector

It seems that one of the lay male rectors was celebrating his fifty-sixth birthday. He intended to keep it secret, but somehow one of the students discovered the date. All of a sudden on the bulletin board of the hall a sign appeared with a Happy Birthday greeting. As might be expected in a lively dorm, various messages were added to the sign—not disrespectful, just male banter.

The rector happened to be standing in front of the sign and reading some of the notes when one of the ROTC juniors came by and asked him how old he really was. The rector responded, "I am fifty-six today, and almost old enough to be your grandfather!" The student answered in return, "That's okay, as long as you are young enough to be my friend." As the student headed to the stairwell to go up to his room, he called out, "Happy Birthday!" Little did he realize what a wonderful gift he had already given the rector.

The Stay-Hall System

Starting in fall 1965, Notre Dame moved away from its long-established tradition of assigning residence halls to particular classes of undergraduates. Instead of moving every year, the students now spend their entire four years in the same dormitory. In the eyes of some alumni the new stay-hall system has been seen as an attack upon class loyalty. While it has some impact on the number of students who know each other in the same undergraduate cohort, they can extend their network of friends beyond the dorm through class-based activities and contacts with upperclass men and women in their coursework.

As a longtime resident of Sorin Hall, I can say from firsthand experience that the stay-hall system has worked immensely well. It is particularly helpful to the rectors since it provides a longer time frame within which they can get to know the young women and men entrusted to their care. They can accompany them through three or four years and develop relationships that often blossom into lifelong friendships. In addition, the presence of three classes of campus-conditioned students makes the transition for the incoming ones much smoother. Residence halls made up entirely of first-year students were a huge challenge to the rectors, since everybody was going through the same set of transitions at the same time. At its best, an undergraduate dormitory can reconstitute itself each year as a kind of community that replicates the life and activity of the broader campus.

One dimension of the stay-hall system that is fraught with some anxiety is the process each spring by which the students within a dorm, by class, determine their roommates for the following year. In women's dorms, choosing one's roommates and circle of friends seems to assume a higher priority and urgency than it usually does in the male dorms. My six female relatives who attended Notre Dame all would attest that room-pick time is full of pressure, some fear, and a fair amount of speculation about motives. For the rector and assistant rector, the period preceding room selections calls for close attention.

Although dorms pick by class, they use different standards to determine the order of the room picks. In the past it was often by grade-point average, but currently it is usually a randomized computer-generated lottery using ID numbers. In some dorms the rooms vary from singles to quints. Others have a pretty steady allotment of doubles, but then location and proximity become big priorities. Usually a master grid of the dorm is placed outside of the rector's office for residents to examine and use as a basis for their individual and collective decision-making. Sometimes the upperclass students drop water balloons from above onto the freshmen while they await their turn. From the rector's point of view, the biggest problem occurs when no one seems to want to room with a particular student.

The whole intent of room picks is to maximize choice in the undergraduate residence halls. Generally the system works well. But human nature fears a vacuum, and perhaps the greatest vacuum of all is not to be able to determine with any reliability with whom one will be living for each of one's precious undergraduate years.

STUDENT LIFE

Lyons Hall and the Elephant

A number of years ago, when Lyons Hall was still all-male, a campus-wide tug-of-war across a large mud pit was announced. Some students in Lyons Hall decided that they would figure out a way to guarantee that they would win the contest. They went to Peru, Indiana, which bills itself as the "circus capital of the world," and rented an elephant. When the other dorms heard than an elephant had arrived on campus, the Lyons team was moved right to the championship round. Another team, as a last-ditch effort, rented a truck. They thought that would give them an equal chance against the elephant, but then they discovered that elephants are able to tear bumpers off trucks and cars. With that in mind,

and lest they be charged a double fee for losing the bumper, they decided to play it straight and just compete as humans.

One of the participants from the Lyons side later described with great glee the image of the elephant, accompanied by the students from Lyons Hall, slowly but surely dragging the opposing team through the mud pits. The moral of this story is "plan ahead."

A Naive Freshman

I came to Notre Dame as a student in the academic year of 1959–60. On one hand, having grown up in Washington, D.C., and having survived Archbishop John Carroll High School and the city's playgrounds, I thought that I was ready for anything. On the other hand, I was eager to get off to a good start and not make any foolish mistakes early on. I lived in Farley Hall next door to the North Dining Hall. A few days into the first week of school, I moved along the line waiting for lunch. When I got to the person who was checking IDs and was striking our names off the master list for each meal, he asked me why I had been missing breakfast: "Don't you know that you're required to go to all meals unless you have special permission?" I thought that this sounded odd, but I didn't want to antagonize him. He added, "I'm afraid I'm going to have to ask you to go visit Father Micelli to get his permission for missing breakfast."

Despite my misgivings, I dutifully knocked on Father Micelli's door that evening. When he invited me in, I said, "I've come to get a letter giving me permission for missing breakfast at the dining hall." He looked at me, as only an experienced rector could, and asked, "Who told you that you couldn't miss breakfast?" I replied, "The checker at the dining hall told me that I had to get permission from you." Without batting an eye, he wrote a brief note, sealed the envelope, and gave it to me.

The next morning I proceeded along the line and saw the checker in his accustomed place. I was just about a person or two removed when he laughed and said, "I hope you didn't take me seriously yesterday." In my heart of hearts I mumbled "I hate you," but I was outwardly nonplussed and merely smiled. When I got back to my room, I opened the note: "To Whom It May Concern: I give permission for Edward Malloy to miss breakfast. He seems like a nice young man." It was signed Matthew Micelli, C.S.C.

Now, looking back, I can't believe that I was so naive. Yet I'm willing to acknowledge that prudence is the better part of valor, especially when you're beginning your college career.

The Sorin Statue

The statue of Father Edward Sorin, C.S.C., lies straight south of the Main Building looking down Notre Dame Avenue. It has an honored place among the iconography on campus. But there is a half-sized version of the same statue that has had an intriguing history. When I was an undergraduate, I first learned about the smaller statue appearing on postcards sent from various places around the world. It was said to have almost a will of its own, although everyone knew this was an ongoing student prank.

I remember vividly two incidents in which the statue appeared dramatically. The first took place on the bank of St. Mary's Lake near the Grotto. Word had gone out across the campus the day before that Sorin would appear at a certain time and place, and so a fairly large crowd had gathered to see what would happen. Near the appointed hour we could see off in the distance on the lake a rowboat with a figure astride. As the boat got closer, it became evident that the statue had been lashed to the middle and no one was on board. It turned out that someone had rigged up a small motor in the rear that was guided by remote control. As the boat came up to the shore, everyone cheered in unison. Edward Sorin had returned home once again! The second took place at halftime during one of the football games. To the accompaniment of the Notre Dame Marching Band, a helicopter circled the stadium and lowered Sorin in a net, much to the delight of all present.

Then, the Sorin statue disappeared. There were rumors about who might have purloined it and where it was concealed. As usually happens in such cases, the word finally leaked out that the statue was being kept in the basement of a Notre Dame graduate who, it turns out, was one of my undergraduate classmates and friends. Under dire threats about revoking his degree, he returned the statue to campus where it was kept in the room of one of the Holy Cross priests. For several years it remained in relative seclusion.

Finally, the time came for an extensive renovation of Sorin Hall. For much of one summer, the whole basement area was completely redone, new stairwells were built, and other major alterations were made. The then-rector of the hall decided to seek the statue's return to its namesake dormitory. This was agreed to with the proviso that the statue be secured from further theft. The hollow interior was filled with concrete and a steel rod was inserted, which was connected to the floor immediately outside the room of the rector. After some testing, the word got out that the statue was impregnable to attack.

Meanwhile, a new tradition developed in the dormitory. It was said that if any student touched the toes and the nose of the statue each day, he (or she) was guaranteed to be graduated in four years. Despite the fact that our students are more religious than is true on most college campuses and seem oblivious to the

appeal of superstition, each class of entering students in the dorm was initiated in the rite of rubbing the toes and the nose. In fact, you could sit outside the rector's office during the span of a day and find a good percentage of the dorm participating in this ritual of assurance, similar to rubbing Saint Peter's toe in the Vatican for good luck.

With the passage of time, one of the sons of the classmate who had hidden the statue in his basement became a student in Sorin Hall. He told me on his first day in the dorm, after his family had left, that it was his call in life to emulate the behavior of his father and find a way, before he graduated, of regaining control of the statue. I did notice, on several occasions, this young man hovering around it looking for a point of vulnerability. Nevertheless, he moved on to his graduation with nary a sign of his being able to follow in his father's footsteps. During Commencement weekend I had a brief conversation with father and son and told them that I was hopeful that they could let mere memories of the temporary possession of the statue suffice. There are no guarantees that the half-size version of the statue will never take another journey, but since it serves such an important role in the lives of contemporary students, it would be contrary to the common good if Father Sorin ever left home again.

Andrew and His Parents

Andrew, a handsome young man from Milwaukee, had had a limited amount of experience. when he came to Notre Dame. A couple of weeks into his first year as an undergraduate he went to a party on Notre Dame Avenue. He drank a little too much and upon exiting the house missed the step off the porch and landed on a hard surface on his jaw. Because of the effects of the alcohol, he didn't feel the pain at first. But when he went back to his dorm he eventually had to go to the Student Health Center, which sent him down to the emergency room at the hospital.

It turned out that Andrew had broken his jaw in six places. His parents came into town to visit him at the hospital, where he was in constant pain. They were immediately supportive and did everything they could to minimize the impact upon his personal and educational life during this first year of college. For the next six months he was forced to eat pureed food through a straw. He lost some weight, but after the jaw healed he was able to return to his former self.

A couple of months after all of this had transpired, Andrew came by the room of his rector to deliver a plant that he had purchased from one of the local florists. This was to thank the rector for his involvement during Andrew's time of difficulty, but the young man also indicated that he had never realized how much his parents loved him until he found himself in such a difficult scrape. There is nothing more inspiring about Notre Dame than to see relationships grow between parents and children. It is unfortunate that sometimes the bonds between them are only acknowledged when they are put to the test.

From a Fracture to Food
for the Homeless

This is a story about Lisa, a young Notre Dame student. One night she was waiting with her boyfriend outside the Joyce Center for football tickets. At a certain point she decided to run across the street to get something to drink and was hit by a car. When the ambulance arrived, she was taken to the hospital where it was determined that she had a broken leg. Her parents were traveling at the time, but eventually they were found and gave permission for the doctors to perform surgery on her leg.

Lisa wore a cast for a couple of months. This was obviously unpleasant and cumbersome, but finally her leg healed and the cast was removed. She decided that she wanted a small private Mass with fifteen of her closest friends to thank God for saving her life. The incident had helped her look more deeply into her values, and as a result she had changed her priorities. She was searching for some way to manifest this new sense of self.

Every time she ate in the dining hall, Lisa had noticed that a substantial amount of food was wasted, partly as a result of students putting too much on their plates and not eating it all. She decided to remedy the situation. First, she composed a letter urging students to take only as much food as they could eat. Second, she developed a means by which the extra food that had been saved could be brought to the Hope Rescue Mission to feed the homeless. This project, which required the use of one of the Center for the Homeless vans, quickly became institutionalized. Over time, food was provided not only for the Hope Rescue Mission but also for other worthy recipients in the South Bend community. This is a great example of how something painful and negative can be transformed into an opportunity to make a positive difference in the well-being of others.

The Elevator and My Seminar

In the spring of 2002, as usual, I taught my first-year seminar in Room 500 of the Main Building. We meet on Sunday nights from 7 to 9:30, and, when class ends, all of my students leave together and have the same destination: the bank of elevators.

About five or six weeks into the seminar, Margaret Smee, the night monitor in the Main Building where the students have to check in on Sunday nights, shared with me her concern that all eighteen members of the class were getting on the same elevator to come down to the ground floor. She was worried that they were putting themselves at risk if the elevator could not handle the load, and she gently encouraged them to use two separate elevators. But by that time in the semester the class had a certain espirit de corps symbolized by their descent as a group.

I mulled over my options. On the one hand, I tried to figure out how much the class collectively must weigh. Many of the women and some of the men were rather slim in build, none was gigantic in height or breadth. I thought to myself that I didn't want to squelch their enthusiasm or seem to be too much of a nag. On the other hand, I wondered whether Margaret's misgivings were legitimate. I, too, did not want to risk the class members' safety. After several weeks of inaction, I finally decided to check with Margaret once again. It turned out that she had called the people in the Maintenance Office who are responsible for the elevators. They had informed her that if at any point the elevator got overloaded, a bell would sound and it simply wouldn't move.

When the day of the final class came, I hovered around the classroom door after my students had all picked up their papers and had made their way to the elevator. With glee, they waited until all eighteen were on board; then the door shut and the elevator made its way down to the exit floor. I was happy that I had not said anything since they had made up a special tradition on their own. They were so comfortable with one another that they enjoyed being crammed together for at least a few minutes each night after class. Sometimes you can have fun in the simplest of ways.

The Badin Hall Christmas Tree

During my senior year at Notre Dame in 1962–63, I served as president of Badin Hall. As the holiday season approached, I asked several students to purchase a Christmas tree to be placed on the porch of the second floor of the dorm. The students who undertook this task decided that they would pursue the cheapest route to getting a tree. They looked around the campus and discovered a well-developed and symmetrical row of evergreens along the broad driveway in front of what was then called Dujarie Institute (now Carroll Hall).

Adept thieves that they were, they cut down a tree, which was fairly large, and dragged it from Dujarie along the lake directly to Badin Hall. The well-trained Notre Dame police arrived at the scene of the crime and proceeded, Sherlock Holmes–like, to follow the path in the snow directly to the dorm. When they glanced up on the porch, they saw a Christmas tree about the same size as the one that was missing. They proceeded to inform the rector, Father Joseph Garvin, C.S.C., that a theft had been committed and they needed to hold someone responsible.

Father Garvin was a short, white-haired, unpretentious priest who was a medieval scholar and assistant director of the Medieval Institute. He was a wonderful priest, but somewhat shy, and spoke with a soft voice. He told the police officers that he would contact the brothers at Dujarie and assured them that restitution would be made. Not wanting to make a scene, the officers withdrew and left the matter in the hands of Father Garvin. Then Father Garvin called me in, as hall president, and indicated his displeasure. He said that he would confer with the brother superior of Dujarie and agree upon the terms of settlement. I said that we would cover the cost of a new tree from the hall treasury but, in the light-hearted spirit of Christmas, suggested that we might couple a new tree with the celebration of Arbor Day. And thus it turned out.

On Arbor Day, a group of students from the dorm walked in procession from Badin Hall down to the road around the lakes and wended their way over to Dujarie. Behind them came a four-wheeled vehicle carrying a large tree with its roots encased in soil. At the end of the procession was Father Garvin in his liturgical robes, including a cope, the vestment worn for benediction. When we arrived at the place where the evergreen had been cut down and a new hole had been dug, we were greeted by the local superior and several brother candidates. As I remember the event, I said a few words indicating our embarrassment at having been caught cutting down one of the prize trees in front of the dorm. Then the hall poet proceeded to recite Joyce Kilmer's familiar poem, "Trees." At its conclusion there was a round of applause. Then Father Garvin, with due solemnity, read a few prayers, offered a blessing, and then sprinkled the tree to be planted. At the end of the ceremony there was another round of applause from all involved.

The Dining Halls

For much of its modern history, Notre Dame has gotten by with two dining halls—North and South. The South Dining Hall has an older pedigree and was built at the same period as Dillon and Alumni Halls. It has stood the test of time and reminds many visitors to its east and west sections of the scenes from the Harry Potter movies when the kids are gathered in British boarding-school splendor. The Holy Cross community used to eat at one end on an elevated platform where they could look out over the assembled students. I have been told that the same priests and brothers would sit next to each other day after day and year after year. It was one element of the French boarding-school tradition that lingered on after the Main Building was no longer the center of all campus activities. More recently, the South Dining Hall has been renovated and expanded. Food options have been multiplied manyfold and a new eating area has been added in the back.

The North Dining Hall was built in the 1950s, and when I was a student it reminded me of what we would now call Motel 6 architecture. It was simple and unpretentious, a place where one did not expect too much in the way of culinary delights and where most of the students didn't linger too long. After it was renovated, it became more attractive on the outside and provided more serving options on the inside. In the main section, when all of the sliding doors are pulled back for large-scale celebratory meals, it reminds me of the main deck of a large ocean liner like the *Queen Mary*.

For the students who are accustomed to a wide variety of food and drink from their home life, even the best grows stale after awhile. Alumni from decades ago can't imagine how the students of today could have any reason for complaint. They recall the days of limited options, one glass of milk, and precise hours of serving. Yet, there is at least one benefit from the occasional expressions of discontent in the student newspaper. It really would not serve any good purpose for the undergraduates to return home bragging about how they ate better at school than they do when they are with their families. .

Now, with flex points and different meal plans, students can eat regularly, not only in one of the two dining halls but also in the various food outlets in LaFortune Student Center and some of the academic buildings. Hours have been extended, so students can order a grab-and-go to take with them if they have a short timespan between classes or activities. The folklore about the "Freshman 15," referring to how many pounds students often put on in their first year of college, is more a function of the extracurricular eating habits of the students—orders from pizza and fast-food vendors—than what is regularly provided for them in nutrition-sensitive dining halls. It is also a result of their hectic lifestyles, the availability of beer and other alcoholic beverages, and their quick physical maturation. All in all, the sharing of food among friends is still one of the best ways to cultivate friendships and celebrate the wonders of the college years.

A Late-Night Trip to the Health Center

Some time ago, I was celebrating an end-of-the-year dinner with one of my undergraduate seminars. We had gathered in a university-owned facility off campus and had enjoyed a good meal, reflection about the experiences of the semester, and a rousing game of Scattergories. During the course of the evening one of my women students seemed to be suffering some significant discomfort and pain. Afterward, I asked her if there was anything I could do to help. She told me that she had a chronic back problem and probably should pay a visit to the University Health Center. I volunteered to drive her there and to stay with her until some diagnosis was made.

I was dressed informally when the two of us arrived at the Health Center and checked in with the woman at the main desk. I informed her of the student's plight, and she soon took her to one of the examination rooms where a nurse on night duty began to tend to her. Meanwhile, I was lingering in the area next to the desk and, since the evening was quiet with not much activity, I began to converse with the check-in attendant.

After a couple of minutes of non-consequential conversation, she asked if I worked at Notre Dame. I said that I did and left it at that. A few moments later she asked if I was on the faculty. Again, I said yes. To keep the conversation going, she then wondered how many courses I taught. I replied that I usually taught one course per semester. She observed that that seemed like a low teaching load. After a long pause, she asked whether I did anything else at the university. I responded that I was also in the administration. Then, after another long pause, she asked what position I held. I said that I was president of Notre Dame. For a second it looked as though she had been struck with apoplexy, but she explained that she was relatively new on the job and did not really know much about the administration. I said that it was no big deal, and soon after the student emerged from the examination room with some painkillers to get her through the night. I then drove her back to the dorm and returned to my residence in Sorin Hall.

The next day I received an apologetic call from Annie Thompson, the director of the Health Center. She told me that her staff were collectively appalled that I had not been recognized. I repeated that it was no big deal and that the student and I were both well treated at the check-in desk. Of course it is more important to receive good service than to be recognized, but from subsequent conversations, I learned that now, right below the check-in area but out of the sight of visitors, are photographs of the major officers of the university with their names. In the years since, I have noticed an almost excessively solicitous attention whenever I have visited the Health Center for minor medical problems of my own.

Inside the Dome

During the summer after my junior year in college, the university was in the process of regilding the Golden Dome on top of the Main Building, which takes place about every twenty years. The process itself is not complicated, but in order to do it safely the university needs to erect a large scaffolding that literally covers the outside Dome itself. On a lark, one of my classmates, Tom Schlereth, and I decided to see if we could get up into the top of the Dome. Some of the usual security efforts were relaxed because of the regilding project.

One summer evening, when things were quiet in the Main Building, Tom and I made our way to one of the stairwells and climbed around the barrier that prevented access to the fifth floor. At first we were a bit startled because at that time the university kept some of its sculpture collection in a large open area on that floor. We were feeling somewhat guilty already, and as we turned a corner we saw an outline of a human form. It took us a few seconds to recognize that it was a clay bust.

Having survived that scare, we found the spiral staircase that took us up to the area immediately outside the walkway around the inside of the Dome. After exploring further, we reached a hidden stairwell that went up into the dark interior above the inner Dome. We had come well prepared with flashlights. This section of the building has large wooden arches supported by the exterior walls. On top of the inner Dome is a ladder that rises up to the base area of the statue of the Blessed Virgin. The ladder itself is a bit shaky, but with proper care one can climb up to the base itself. At that point, some boards have been laid across the base, less than a floor but more than just a few isolated pieces of lumber. Once we got our footing, we were standing approximately at the height of the wooden louvers just below the statue itself. We opened the louvers and looked out at the grand view of the campus.

The statue is hollow and rises to about seventeen feet. Depending on one's girth, you can shimmy up inside the statue about two-thirds of the way. At the top of the statue is a lightning rod that allows a little bit of sunlight or moonlight to provide some illumination. The proof that one had ascended to that point was to steal a packet or two of the gold leaf intended for the exterior of the Dome and statue. Tom and I enjoyed ourselves immensely as we examined the intricacy of the statue and looked out over the silent campus. Eventually we made our way down across the inner Dome and then down the ladder to the floor outside of the inner mural. In order to commemorate our visit we wrote in chalk, "Monk and Scoop [our nicknames] were here."

Such was my first venture inside the statue. Many years later, when I was on the staff of Moreau Seminary and Father Jerry Wilson, C.S.C., was about to retire as vice president of Business Affairs, I talked him into allowing me to host a group of seventeen seminarians for a daytime tour up inside the Dome and statue. Father Wilson was not by temperament a daring person, and I was surprised he gave us permission.

On the day of his retirement we had the keys to get past the various barriers. Because it was the in middle of a workday, we tried to do it as inconspicuously as possible. Gradually we made our way up on the same path that Tom and I had taken when we were seniors. The first problem was that the ladder up into the top of the inner Dome goes through a rather narrow place. One of the seminarians was too heavy to make it, so he was forced to stay behind, but the other sixteen all made it up eventually. The second problem happened when, one by one, the seminarians were going up inside the statue and coming back down to the top of the inner Dome. One of the young men was about halfway up the ladder into the base when he froze. I called out and told him that if he didn't keep going I would prod him all the way up. After a bit of hesitation he completed his trip to the top and made his way back down. Another seminarian, who was standing in the base of the statue, inadvertently hit a board, which fell and clanged off the top of the inner Dome. I am sure that someone must have heard the noise, but no one reported it.

Finally, everyone made it back down to the lower floors of the Main Building with no further difficulty. It turned out to be a guided tour much prized by those who had had a chance to enjoy it. In later years, other students would periodically find a way to get past the barriers. Unfortunately, at a certain point some damage was done, and the university put in place a relatively foolproof system to prevent any more unauthorized expeditions inside the Dome.

No Price Too High

It seems that a pair of identical twins once were graduated from Notre Dame. When they began their professional careers, they ended up some distance from each other. One lived and worked in Amsterdam, the Netherlands, and the other in Alaska. Both of them were rabid Notre Dame football fans and desirous of keeping up with the outcome of every game. It turned out that the twin in Amsterdam had no access by television or radio to the game as it unfolded. In desperation, he called on his cell phone to his brother in Alaska and proceeded to stay on the line during the whole course of the match. He thought it a small price to pay for a play-by-play account. Someone once said that when you are indoctrinated into the Notre Dame family, for the rest of your adult life you will never rest content on a Saturday in the fall until you know how the Fighting Irish have done.

Umbrella Machismo

I went through my whole undergraduate career without ever owning an umbrella. It is true that in cold weather I did wear a parka so that I was able to protect myself from the elements by putting my hood up. But in the fall and spring when the weather was pleasant, I simply dashed from building to building or pretended that there was no precipitation, even during downpours. As a result, I can understand why the majority of contemporary male students seem to be imitating the example of myself and my peers. In the heaviest rainstorms, to make a mad dash seems a way of losing face. So they get soaked as if it didn't matter, even if they are on the way to class, where they'll have to sit in wet clothes for the duration of the lecture.

Women students have more common sense. A high percentage own umbrellas and use them since they perceive no disgrace in protecting themselves from the weather. But if they are in the company of men students and don't want to seem excessively dainty, they don't raise their umbrellas, even if they are carrying them.

On those days when the temperature hovers near freezing and a leaden cold rain falls, students become sitting ducks for colds, flu, and other ailments. It is absolutely predictable that the Health Center will be full of sniffling and coughing young people at these times of year. Maybe it is simply the way of youth to ignore the advice that their parents give them. It reminds me of those male students when the weather is frigid who go without shirts during football games and paint a message on their bare chests. The colder it gets, the more they can rely on the television cameras zooming in on them during the course of the game. I'm sure their parents, if they watch from home, wonder whether they are wasting their tuition money—but perhaps they remember their own college days.

Wipeout

I was walking in front of Sacred Heart Basilica when all of a sudden a young male student wiped out his bicycle and lay sprawling across the cement. When he looked up and saw who I was, he apologized for swearing. Then he determined that he probably hadn't broken any bones, even though he had a minor abrasion on one of his hands. If he had not been so young and agile, he probably would have done serious damage to himself.

In the best and worst senses of modern life, his first concern was not for his physical well-being, but for his laptop computer. As he got up from the ground, he patted the exterior of the carrying case and opened it up with some trepidation. Nothing seemed to have been damaged. By this time he decided that he was probably late for class. If he had been in high school, he said, he would have asked me for a note to give to the teacher. Both of us decided that that would not be appropriate. Then he thanked me for worrying about him, got back on the bike and rode off. I was left wondering whether, if he had broken a bone, he would have given the same careful attention to his laptop computer while awaiting an ambulance.

Ring the Right Doorbell

It was the month of November, and a group of undergraduates were seen by Notre Dame Security walking near the Alumni/Senior Club. One of the students, when he saw the police car, took off in a mad dash and jumped over the courtyard fence. It wasn't evident to the patrolmen why he did so. After he was pursued, he kept trying to elude the police and eventually disappeared. Later that night, Notre Dame Security received a report from the South Bend police that a student had appeared at the door of the then vice president of Student Affairs, Patricia O'Hara, whose residence is near the St. Joseph River. After he rang the doorbell, she looked out her window and saw a totally soaked male individual and proceeded to call the police. They found the young man shivering in the cold and completely drenched.

The Notre Dame officer who had originally been involved in the case arranged for the student to be transported back to the campus when the South Bend officers did not press charges. The young man was obviously intoxicated. Even after he sobered up a bit, he had no recollection of what had led him to that part of the city or why he had ended up in the river. Little did he know that he had rung the doorbell at Vice President O'Hara's house. Fortunately for all concerned, the student was eventually brought back to his dorm, and the rector was informed of the details of his evening misadventures.

Stolen Bike

It was 4:15 p.m. on a gray Thursday in November when a 6-foot 4-inch, 240-pound freshman knocked on the rector's door and wanted to talk. He began by recounting how his bike had been stolen a few days earlier. On his way back from class he had spotted it anchored to a bike rack in front of a dorm on the other side of the campus. He called Campus Security, who promptly met him at the scene. They inquired whether he had registered his bike with Security or if he knew its serial number.

The student replied that he had grown up on a wheat farm in eastern Washington state, that his family did not lock their home, that keys were left in the ignition of vehicles and farm equipment, and that he did not even know that bikes had serial numbers. Campus Security then explained that they would cut the lock and keep the bike for a week. If no one then claimed the bike, they would turn it over to him.

The student told the rector that it was a run-of-the-mill bike, nothing special. He had had it for several years and knew every scratch on it. He had brought the bike with him to campus in August. Perhaps a bit of homesickness contributed to the tears welling in the corners of his eyes, but he continued without a pause, "Father, this is the first time in my life that someone has not taken me at my word. I suppose that when you leave home, you leave your reputation behind you."

A Proposal at Cinema 14

It seems that a young couple went together to Cinema 14 on a weekday evening. When they arrived, they were the only ones in the theater. They were enjoying the film when there suddenly was some mechanical malfunction. They sat in the dark together for a moment and then the male student went off to alert the projectionist to the problem. The female student remained in her seat.

After a few minutes she looked up and saw on the screen a series of pictures, first of herself, then of herself with the young man, accompanied by romantic music. Finally, in large script on the screen appeared a proposal of marriage. At this point, the young man, wearing a tuxedo, returned to the theater with a bouquet of red roses. He then knelt down before her and asked her in person. As expected, she accepted. They were married after graduation.

For generations of Notre Dame students, a proposal at the Grotto was thought to be invariably accepted. That is probably still the case. But that does not mean that in the hearts of a number of Notre Dame coeds there isn't a new level of expectation for creativity and romantic persistence.

AROUND THE CAMPUS

Student Tour Guides

During the course of every school year, tens of thousands of people visit the Notre Dame campus. Indeed, it is often described as the second largest tourist attraction in the State of Indiana after the Indianapolis Speedway. Some of the visitors are graduates or individuals who have been to the campus many times in the past, but each year sees many first-timers who come to the university as part of organized tour groups, as prospective students and their parents, as longtime followers of Notre Dame's athletic fortunes, as attendees at special events like weddings and funerals, or just people who happen to be driving down Interstate 80 and spy the exit signs for Notre Dame.

With the construction of the Eck Center, we now have a facility that is attractive and comfortable for new visitors. In the auditorium they can view one of several videos on the history and present realities of the institution. The Eck Center is the starting point for most organized tours of the campus. During the school year, the guides are a dedicated and well-prepared contingent of Notre Dame students who are agents of hospitality as well as privileged storytellers to those who are curious about Notre Dame. I was a tour guide myself as an undergraduate and a member of the Blue Circle Honor Society. I very much enjoyed representing Notre Dame to the outside world. Today the tradition lives on because of the volunteer spirit of so many of our students who take pride in the university and seek to represent it with enthusiasm and conviction.

At the busiest times of year one can see a constant movement of tour guide–led groups of various sizes from two or three persons to forty or fifty. Depending on the amount of time the visitors have available, the guides will lead them around the heart of the old campus and to the centers of academic and athletic life. Just about every tour includes a visit to the Main Building, Sacred Heart Basilica, the Grotto, and the Hesburgh Library. Most also encircle the outside of the football stadium and view the sports memorabilia and photographs in the Joyce

Center. For prospective students, there is also a chance to walk through the Coleman-Morse Center and LaFortune Student Center as well as one of the dining halls. It goes without saying that nearly every visiting group eventually ends up at the Hammes Notre Dame Bookstore.

It should not be surprising that some of the tour guides are inclined to embellish their storytelling with humor and hyperbole. Most of them have ready responses when someone asks about the statue on the top of the Golden Dome. No, it is not Jesus, and it is not Knute Rockne. (It is the Blessed Virgin.) When visitors inquire about the severity of the rules regulating student life, the student guides not only describe parietal hours, single-sex dorms, and the sexual ethics code but also defend them as good things.

I have discovered through the years, especially in the summer when my windows are open, that most guides make reference to the fact that I reside in the turret in Sorin Hall. They like to brag that I both teach undergraduate students and live in a student dormitory. As they walk by Sorin, they usually point to my room on the first floor of the northeast turret. When I am sitting at the desk in my room, I usually wave to the group. They are usually flabbergasted, and many wonder whether the university has created a robotized image of me that moves automatically at the control of the tour guide.

The great value of student tour guides is that they have youthful enthusiasm as well as instant credibility. When they gush about what a great school Notre Dame is or how much they have enjoyed student life, their comments come across as authentic. When they describe how hard Notre Dame undergraduates work and how challenging the classes are, their very articulateness reinforces the truthfulness of their claims. And when the student guides attest to the regular religious practice of so many Notre Dame· undergraduates, it is worth a thousand statistical profiles emanating from Campus Ministry. It has been said that while adults can convey the prose of Notre Dame, only students can convey its poetry.

Sounds of Notre Dame

A modern university reverberates with all the usual sounds that one might identify with large numbers of students full of energy, sociability, and sometimes intense displays of emotion and partisanship. Each morning in the dormitories begins with the hall janitor and maids cleaning the corridors, getting rid of trash, and preparing the living environment for another day of student life. Alarm clocks ring, doors slam, water splatters in the showers, and young people hail each other as they go off to class. In the classrooms, faculty members arrive, students settle in their seats, coats are taken off, and backpacks are laid aside. In the offices, the secretaries usually arrive first, doors are opened, lights are turned on, greetings are exchanged, schedules are reviewed, and coffee is brewed for those who need a kick-start to the day. In the ECDC daycare facility, young children from age two on up are dropped off by their parents, and their youthful voices can be heard chattering in the hallways and in the playground in the rear. In the support and maintenance areas, trucks are loaded with gear and workers prepare for the day. On the warm days of late spring, summer, and fall, the lawnmowers begin their appointed rounds at a hectic pace of whirring and clipping. Meanwhile, delivery trucks back up with bleeps to alert any unwary pedestrian. On the lakes, the ducks, geese, and swans can be heard quacking and honking as they land on the water in elegant splashes. Occasionally, a stray dog or cat will disrupt their routines and generate anguished complaints from the lakeside fowl.

In the winter, after the arrival of snow, energetic crews sweep the campus clean, roads and pedestrian paths alike. One can hear the squishing of boots on the new-fallen cover and the endless screeching of steel blades that push aside the snow and ice. On the night of the first significant snowfall, especially if the conditions are ideal, one can hear the sounds of small groups of students engaging in a spontaneous snowball fight, one side of the campus against the other.

During Freshman Orientation Week, new students decked out in the appropriate colored T-shirt chant the supremacy of their newfound homes in the halls. Early in the mornings, one can hear some of the ROTC units as they make their way in step around the lakes to laundered versions of old military marching songs. And then the newly constituted Notre Dame marching band makes its way around the campus for the first time in the academic year, playing all the old university favorites with a special thrill attached to the greatest of all fight songs, "The Notre Dame Victory March."

On home football weekends, when the campus is enlarged by almost 80,000 visitors, the range of sounds displays its greatest variety. Those manning eating stations spread around the quads hawk their wares, sometimes over megaphones. Bagpipers and auto horns play the "Victory March" while little kids squeal and old grads brag about the days of yore. The Notre Dame band enthralls its audience with the pre-game show on the steps of Bond Hall. Then they march to the stadium in uniform amid cheering crowds. Sometimes a police helicopter flies overhead, or one hears the sirens of police and fire vehicles as they respond to an emergency or speed the arrival of visiting teams and visitors of note.

Setting the temporal tone for all of this campus activity are the bells of Sacred Heart Basilica. From 10 a.m. to 10 p.m. they ring out on the quarter hour and reach their climax with the four bells signaling the passage of an hour and the following bells striking the time. At the conclusion of each day of bell ringing, the tower gives forth with the "Alma Mater," signaling the institution's devotion to Mary the Mother of Jesus. On the days when Holy Cross religious die and there is a funeral Mass in the Basilica, the bells toll with odd syncopation to evoke a spirit of mourning and reflection. Before each Mass, and on special days of liturgical celebration, the multiple bells of Sacred Heart joyfully peal throughout the surrounding countryside.

The sounds of Notre Dame are the cheers of its loyal fans, the joy of its youthful students, the movement of vehicles and people to their destinations. The sounds of Notre Dame are friends calling each other by name, bull sessions in the dorms in the darkness of night, and consolation found in the quiet of the Grotto. In the last analysis, the sounds of Notre Dame are simply a reverberation of its people at work—a community of teachers and learners at prayer, at service, and at study.

Gate Cons

Because Notre Dame is primarily a pedestrian campus, the university makes every effort to restrict access for automobiles and trucks. The members of the security operation who staff the two gates have an extremely difficult job. On the one hand, they want to provide a fitting greeting, clear instructions, and an appropriate introduction to the campus. On the other hand, they want to keep out those who are trying to beat the system or avoid a long walk. Students, especially, are tempted to concoct one excuse or another to bring a car on campus in order to drop off a friend or to bring beer or other items to their dorms. Here are several anecdotes.

One story began at the Main Gate around 3 a.m. The bar crowd was heading back to the campus, and the security guard was handed all the usual excuses from "I need to drop off my date," to "my buddy isn't feeling too good." As the vehicular traffic cleared out, the guard noticed five male students walking on Notre Dame Avenue and heading for the gate. They were walking in a formation of sorts and had arranged themselves as if they were riding in a car—driver and front-seat passenger, then two guys carrying the third as if all three were in the back seat. They were in the northbound lane of Notre Dame Avenue, stopped at the intersection, and then continued in a left-turn arc toward the entrance lane of the Main Gate. The security guard stepped out of the gatehouse as the "driver" pretended to roll down the window. He asked if he could "drive" onto campus because his friend "in the backseat" was too ill to walk. The guard played along by asking some questions that really made the "driver" smile. Finally, he gave them the go-ahead and raised the gate. With that, they erupted in laughter and cheers.

At 5 a.m. on a Sunday, a male student approached the gate wanting to go to Mass. He had on a nice jacket and dress shirt. He looked as though he had just awakened or perhaps had never gone to bed the night before. As he approached the window, the guard could see that below the waist he was wearing a pair of floral-print boxer shorts and flip-flops. Since there was no scheduled five o'clock morning Mass, he was refused entry.

A student pulled up to the gate and asked to take his lady friend to the Health Center since she was having "labor pains." She had stuffed a lopsided pillow under her shirt. The guard advised them to call an ambulance since there is no doctor in the Health Center after hours. They declined and drove off.

A student in a station wagon asked to drive to his dorm to drop off some miscellaneous items. The guard looked over and saw a large lump of something covered with a green blanket. He could discern that there was a person under the blanket since a sneaker was sticking out. The guard told him that there was no need to drive in since the items had just grown legs and could now walk under their own power.

A security officer working the East Gate on the early morning shift noted a car approaching very slowly. The officer stepped out of the gatehouse and greeted the driver, who was obviously annoyed. When the officer asked if he could help, the driver said several times, "Just give me my ticket." The officer asked where he needed to go, and he replied, "To Chicago." After another short exchange it became clear that the driver thought that he had pulled up to the entrance of the Toll Road.

A number of years ago, the daughter of one of the university's vice presidents was on duty at one of the gates as a graduate student. One morning a young lady approached the gate and told the daughter, not knowing that she was related, that she wanted to see the vice president. The daughter replied that she was sorry, but the vice president was not in that day. The woman then told the student not to speak for the vice president and to open the gate. Growing more and more impatient, she demanded, "How do you know that he is not available?" The student replied, "Well, he happens to be my father, and I know he is out of town." The woman made a right turn and was never seen again.

In the old days, the Main Gate was often used as a punishment for students before the time of coeducation. Priest rectors would often have young men in trouble report to the Main Gate every hour on the hour during the night and sign in with the officer until daybreak, when they were then expected to appear at Mass.

In the early 1980s a man approached the Main Gate and said that he had to drop something off at the Main Building. The guard rightly asked if the item was large and cumbersome. The man replied that it was large but not particularly cumbersome. The guard then asked him to just park in the main circle and walk over to the Main Building. Only later did he discover that the man happened to be Colonel Frederick B. Snite, and he was dropping off a two-million-dollar check for the building of the Snite Museum of Art. Mr. Snite never told the guard who he was or sought any special privileges.

Some students regularly try to beat the system to get on campus. One student kept a dorm-size refrigerator in the back seat of his car as a perpetual excuse. Another had a fake cast that he tossed into the back seat as he went to class, and a few students have purchased clerical collars in order to gain admittance. One student even went to work as a local pizza deliveryman to obtain the company hat and shirt in order to be able to drive on campus.

Campus Waterfowl

As far as I know, it was not recorded what kind of waterfowl inhabited St. Joseph's and St. Mary's Lakes on campus when Father Sorin first arrived in 1842. I am rather confident that there were ducks of one kind or another. In the experience of those people now alive, one of the fondest memories of campus life has been enjoying the beauty of the lakesides and the antics of the ducks and various birds native to the area. On a quiet weekend in the spring, summer, or fall, who hasn't watched families with little kids feeding the ducks and otherwise enjoying themselves along the lakesides? A Korean couple who were graduate students in the 1970s and lived in the University Village for married students once told me that some of their happiest days at Notre Dame had to do with the ducks on the lake as well as the chipmunks and squirrels and the cardinals flying around.

About ten years ago the lakes became overrun with Canada geese, a protected species. Because they were fed hundreds of times per day, the geese abandoned their nomadic ways and hunkered down on campus. Once they produced offspring, there was even greater motivation to stay put. From a casual observation of the Notre Dame geese's daily routine, it seems to consist primarily in eating, defecating, and chasing joggers and little children.

As the numbers of geese continued to increase, several people sought a solution to the problem. Someone suggested that swans were known to be natural enemies of geese, and a pair of swans was introduced on St. Mary's Lake. At first there were some manifestations of the natural hostility between the two species, but after awhile the swans were distracted by the constant offer of meals by the many visitors to the campus. Before long, it was obvious that the swans and the geese had reached a détente; they simply stayed out of each other's way and life went on. Even when the swans began to have their own offspring, the truce continued. As a result, we now had a problem with too many swans as well as too many geese.

A second solution proposed was to get the Indiana state department that deals with wildlife come and transport the geese away to another location. The first time this move was undertaken, it seemed that we had found the solution to the problem. But then about two or three weeks later, the tribe of geese began to reappear, first in small numbers and then in numbers almost as plentiful as they were before the intervention. A couple of more times through the years we adopted the same strategy, with the same unsatisfactory result.

Every other solution to the problem has been rejected as unworkable. Certain breeds of dogs might be effective in shooing off the geese, but they are also natural enemies of ducks and swans and not always friendly to joggers, walkers, little children, and visitors. If the geese weren't fed so often, they might be inclined to leave, but we can hardly deprive toddlers of the thrill of feeding the wildlife while enjoying the outdoor beauty of the campus.

Meanwhile, life goes on. Each spring the waterfowl population on campus increases when a new generation is born. Some experts claim that the only form of life that would survive a nuclear war is cockroaches. My own suspicion is that the cockroaches would be killed by the still-thriving Canada geese.

Some Campus Trivia

I am not by temperament inclined to remember insignificant facts. In my judgment, trivia should be treated as ephemera, best forgotten unless part of some larger, meaningful pattern. For example, there are some Notre Dame athletic fans who can relate past football games almost moment by moment and play by play. They can recall starting lineups and players whose exploits allowed the Fighting Irish to win. Moreover, there are several books that provide more information about Notre Dame than the average person cares to learn.

Nevertheless, on occasion, especially with new students, I like to pique their curiosity by asking them about some Notre Dame trivia. "How many islands are there on St. Mary's and St. Joseph's Lakes?" The correct answer is that there are two islands on St. Joseph's Lake, which also includes the one approved swimming area, and four on St. Mary's Lake, more than most people usually guess. But, in fact, there are sometimes five islands on St. Mary's when the water level is low. The best way to test these answers is to take a slow walk around each lake.

Another piece of information that the average person does not know is that the area around the two lakes is not all owned by the University of Notre Dame. In 1967, when the university moved to a predominantly lay Board of Trustees, the legal agreement of separation preserved the land north of each of the lakes in perpetual ownership by the Indiana Province of the Congregation of Holy Cross. Thus, on the north side of St. Mary's Lake we have the Fatima Retreat House complex, the parish center for Sacred Heart Parish, Moreau Seminary, and Holy Cross House. Corby Hall, the area around the Grotto, and Columba Hall are also owned by the Indiana Province, although Columba Hall has a long-term lease with the Midwest Province of Holy Cross Brothers.

"How many outdoor basketball courts are there on the campus?" This is a changing reality, since both the bookstore and Stepan Center courts have been torn down. There is one regulation court in the woods adjacent to Carroll Hall; one court northwest of the Stepan Center; three courts just west of the new bookstore, six courts between the nine-hole golf course and McGlinn Hall, and two courts adjacent to Lyons Hall. (See my "Outdoor Basketball" in the next section.)

Here's another one. Since I am the sixteenth president of Notre Dame, why do we have only fourteen portraits of previous administrators in the president's complex on the fourth floor of the Main Building? The answer is that Father William Corby, C.S.C., held office twice. While Notre Dame's presidents have had various lengths of service, only Father Corby, a famous Civil War chaplain, served two presidencies with a gap between them. The statue in front of Corby Hall commemorates his blessing of the Irish Brigade before Pickett's charge on the most decisive day of the conflict at Gettysburg.

Finally, Notre Dame benefits from a large underground aquifer that provides the water for the campus. There are seven wells in the broader campus environment, five of which are being used at any one time. These wells supply water not only for human consumption but also to irrigate the grass, trees, and flowers during the dry seasons of the year.

Keeping the Campus Clean

Notre Dame as an institution has tried to foster some connection between the attractiveness of the physical environment and the invitation to think about fundamental realities and to be in touch with God's presence in the natural order. I am constantly receiving compliments about the beauty of our campus. The trees, the flowers, the grass, the lakefronts, the visual sight lines, and the sense of shared ownership and responsibility are all deeply rooted in our common life.

Twenty years ago a decision was made to place concrete receptacles around the campus for trash and unwanted items. This effort is augmented by small crews who make regular sweeps throughout the grounds to uphold a high standard of cleanliness. It is in this light that I am constantly amazed by what happens on home football weekends. After the expansion of our stadium, we now have on campus more than 80,000 people for each of our six home football weekends. Before, during, and after the game, this multitude leaves behind a significant amount of trash in the stadium and in the surrounding parking lots. But, amazingly, if you take a walk through the heart of the campus immediately after a game, you see that next to each fully loaded trash receptacle is a neat pile of whatever overflow there might be. The rest of the campus tends to be sparklingly clean. By the next morning, when the pickup crews have finished their work, there is literally no evidence that such a large contingent of people was present in the heart of our campus. I have always seen this phenomenon as a kind of metaphor for the relationship between establishing high standards in the first place, making compliance relatively easy and convenient, and passing on a sense of responsibility for the common environment.

Fires at Notre Dame

Father Edward Sorin, C.S.C., and seven Brothers of St. Joseph (as they were then called) founded the University of Notre Dame in 1842. About two miles away was the town of South Bend on the St. Joseph River. The campus property was heavily forested, although there had been some clearing of land along the two lakes. The first buildings were very primitive. Fortunately, the founders possessed the skills necessary to farm the land, provide for basic necessities, and construct what eventually would become a modern university.

Many things went wrong in those early days. The founders were plagued by fetid water- and mosquito-borne diseases, a harsh climate, particularly in winter, financial debts, and occasional hostility from the neighbors. Nevertheless, with perseverance and strong will, more land was cleared, buildings were raised, and the campus began to take shape.

No problem was more destructive and distressing for colleges founded at this time in American history than the ever-present threat of fire. Most buildings were constructed from wood or wood products. Interior heating came from fireplaces and light from candles. Firefighting equipment was almost nonexistent, and any flame that got out of control almost inevitably consumed the whole facility in which it started. Some colleges never recovered from a tragic fire, since few had the resources to rebuild.

Notre Dame was not immune from fire and the destruction that came in its wake. The first major conflagration took place on November 18, 1849. It completely destroyed the apprentice workshops and all the equipment. Father Sorin, in a letter to his superior, Father Basil Moreau, noted, "A line of buildings 130 feet long and two stories high was wiped away by the flames in two hours." Eight years later, in 1857, a fire destroyed the stables, consuming horses, fodder, and farm implements.

In retrospect, the famous fire of 1879 was a decisive moment in the history of Notre Dame. The grand Main Building, which housed most of the central activities of the university, including housing for the students, the library, the dining hall, and the academic classrooms and offices, was destroyed. Father Sorin, no longer president of the university but still superior general of the Holy Cross Congregation, was not present when the fire took place, but he returned quickly to the campus and gathered the community in the main church. In words that would inspire later generations, he proclaimed, "The fire is a sign from the heavens that we have dreamed too small. We will rebuild it even bigger and grander." While other fires have broken out since that time, none has had the potential of the fire of 1879 to destroy the university.

When I was an undergraduate student, I lived in Badin Hall for two years. In my senior year I was hall president. As a kind of joke, one of the members of my administration bore the title "fire commissioner." We knew that if a fire broke out in Badin, we wouldn't have much of a chance. A "fire commissioner" was elected each year after making exaggerated promises about how effective he would be in a crisis. Sometime in the middle of my senior year, while some students were away on a break, a fire broke out in one of the residence hall rooms and set off the fire alarm. Since this was the era before the sprinkler systems, the routine was to unroll the fire hose and to take the axe out of its cabinet and check on whether the fire was serious. The "fire commissioner," as expected, showed up at this critical moment wearing his own version of a helmet and wielding the axe.

We determined, before the Notre Dame Fire Department arrived, that in fact there was a fire in one of the rooms. The "fire commissioner," with a burst of heroic energy, used his axe to break down the door. Several other students manned the hose and sprayed down the room, putting out a fire caused by a paper lantern coming in contact with a hot lightbulb. By the time the Fire Department arrived, all that remained as evidence was the smashed lantern, some ashes of paper that had caught on fire, and some minor smoke damage in the room. The captain thanked both the "fire commissioner" and the other students for their quick action. But he warned them that in the future it would be too risky to take on such a challenge again; he told us that we should leave fire-fighting to the professionals. In retrospect, I am convinced that all of us did the right thing. We probably saved the hall from destruction and validated what otherwise was seen merely to be a humorous addition to hall governance.

Another time, after I had joined the Notre Dame faculty, a fire broke out in the laundry chute in Howard Hall. Father Gene Gorski, C.S.C., was rector at the time. I was alerted by the sound of fire engines on the campus. There was a fair amount of smoke coming out of the roof, the chute serving as a flue. With quick action, the Notre Dame Fire Department quickly brought the flames under control. But what I remember vividly is a rather peaked Father Gorski standing outside the rector's office and saying over and over again, "Be calm. Everything is under control," while his appearance and his gestures suggested just the opposite. Clearly he did the right thing in trying to quell student panic, but his limitations in controlling his own fear was one more reminder of the many challenges of being a Notre Dame rector.

One of the worst fires in the modern era took place on June 25, 1980, when St. Edward's Hall burned to the ground. This took place in the summer, when none of the students were in the dorm and when the only one present was the rector. I learned about the fire after it had been raging for awhile, so when I finally appeared on the scene, it was clear that there was nothing more that the Fire Department could do. A number of area fire departments assisted in fighting the blaze. Ironically, the fire started from some workmen's torches as they began to take down the old fire escapes before activating the new sprinkler system. Once the flames reached the multiple ceilings in the roof, it became impossible to control.

What I remember the most about the St. Edward's fire was not the terrible destruction of the hall, but its aftermath. There were different pockets of people spread around the dorm who were watching the fire as it took place. As soon as the fire chief declared it over, I noticed Father Hesburgh talking to some journalists. Like Father Sorin before him, he promised that we would quickly rebuild and, reflecting his confidence in his staff, he left for the airport and a planned trip. Nearby was a group of administrators involved in the fund-raising side of the university who were already planning how we might effectively raise money from our multiple constituencies to help rebuild the dormitory. Not too far away were people representing the construction, renovation, and other physical plant realities of the institution who were discussing the various steps necessary to close off the building in order to clean up as well as how to house its occupants. Notre Dame is never better than when it faces a severe crisis. Everyone pulls together. As it turned out, St. Edward's Hall was rebuilt and expanded and now is a beautiful and comfortable dorm in the middle of the campus.

Two other major fires in the modern era have taken place during my own term as president. The first destroyed St. Michael's Laundry, next to the Grotto and Brownson and Lewis Halls. One night I was sitting in my room when I heard off in the distance a number of fire trucks coming from South Bend. I turned on my scanner radio and heard the dispatcher say that there was a fire near Brownson and Lewis Halls. As I rushed out of my room, I could smell the acrid smoke in the air. I ran past Sacred Heart Basilica and then down the front of Brownson Hall toward Lewis Hall, where I could see that the laundry was already heavily in flames. There is a little grass knoll between the two buildings, which offered a good view, and I crept closer and closer to its edge. All of a sudden, I found myself slipping down at about a forty-five-degree angle in the direction of the flames. I rode on my rear end straight to the bottom, which put me about five feet from the back wall of the laundry. I could see off to my right that one of the ladder trucks from South Bend was already shooting water into the flames, and I started to run as quickly as I could toward it. I have no idea whether the firefighters saw me, but the last thing in the world I wanted was to be thought a fire bug or somehow implicated in the blaze. Eventually, I made my way over to the Grotto, where the police and fire chiefs had begun to gather with a number of other university administrators. We stood for hours, watching a fire that burned with great intensity. Because there was a heavy wind, embers were being carried up into the air and were threatening a number of other buildings on the campus, including Brownson, Sacred Heart, and the Main Building. Fortunately, the firefighters were able to quench the flames. These were anxious moments, indeed, since we could have lost three or four or five of the most significant buildings on campus. The combined fire crews did a great job in limiting the destruction to St Michael's Laundry.

Most recently, we had to deal with a fire that began at about one o'clock in the morning as a result of an explosion at our power plant. It did several million dollars' worth of damage and threw large pieces of metal considerable distances, including down to the path around St. Mary's Lake. Fortunately, because of the hour when it happened, there was no loss of life, even though two of our employees suffered serious injuries. I was awakened from sleep by one of our Student Affairs officials and hurriedly dressed and made my way to the scene. To this day we do not know, even after an extensive investigation, what caused the explosion. Once again, everybody responded to the situation as effectively as possible so that there was no risk to others and minimum damage to university property.

Through the years I've walked past the scene of the explosion many times on my way back and forth from Moreau Seminary to the campus.

These kinds of events remind us how vulnerable we remain to fire but how fortunate we are to have protective resources that were unavailable to the university's founders. Brother Borromeo Malley, C.S.C., Brother Frank Gorch, C.S.C., and many other Holy Cross brothers have served with distinction on the Notre Dame Fire Department through the years. Now, under the direction of Chief John Antonucci, the department carries on a noble tradition of service.

Campus Scares

In the wake of the events of September 11, 2001, the United States has become aware of the possibility of further terrorist attacks within our country, and citizens have been prompted to be alert to unusual persons, objects, and events. At Notre Dame we had to take these concerns into account even before the tragedy in New York City. In Lou Holtz's first year as football coach, when he started out with a losing record, some high-school kids from town planted a fake bomb in a tree outside the Notre Dame locker room at the football stadium. This seemed to be connected to a series of pranks that went on in the broader community. When Holtz was informed that the security forces had found a device that resembled a bomb, he was quoted as saying, "They must really take football seriously here."

A couple of years ago the security police were patrolling the parking lot adjacent to Moreau Seminary. They discovered at about five o'clock in the morning an old, dirt-covered automobile with anti-war stickers in its windows and on the side. On closer inspection, it was missing a front seat and loose wires were sticking up. The officers decided to rope off the area, close Douglas Road, and call in the bomb squad, who finally determined that there was nothing threatening about the car. A little later, they learned that it was owned by an anti-war activist who happened to be staying as a guest of one of the priests at the seminary.

On September 7, 2004, in the week preceding the anniversary of September 11, Notre Dame Police and Fire Departments were called to LaFortune Student Center for a medical emergency. While they were there, someone pointed out that a strange briefcase had been left off to the side of the student center. It is standard procedure in such circumstances to check the object to determine whether it has the potential to cause harm. A perimeter was established and the South Bend bomb squad was called out. While checking the area for other suspicious objects, someone came upon a brown paper bag in a flower pot near the east entrance of the facility. This led the Police and Fire Departments to extend the perimeter and to evacuate LaFortune. The bomb squad technicians, in full in protective gear, began to examine each of the items. They X-rayed the briefcase and K-9 dogs sniffed it. When it was opened, it contained tools from some kind of kit. When the second package was opened, it was determined that it was a clue in a scavenger hunt. Finally, the all-clear was declared and LaFortune once again was opened up for business. Prior to September 11, 2001, both of the objects would simply have been picked up and brought into the lost-and-found office.

Also in September 2004, Notre Dame Security was dispatched to Wilson Commons in the graduate housing complex. The person entrusted with delivering the mail had heard a ticking sound inside a package. The package's intended recipient could not be located, either at her apartment or at her usual study places. Security decided to cordon off the area and call the South Bend bomb squad. Meanwhile, one of the security officers was able to contact the person who had originally mailed the package and was told that it contained a cordless cell phone and its charger. The bomb squad opened the package and verified the contents, and the opened package was then given to the rector, who returned it to the student. Once more, in the wake of September 11, 2001, and heightened security concerns, the usual procedures were followed. It is a telling reminder of our skittishness and sense of precariousness.

Behind the Scenes

In any complex organization there are individuals who, by job definition and responsibility, are frequently in the public eye. This is true of the president, the vice president of Student Affairs, the deans, the alumni director, the athletic director, and the coaches, especially in the most highly visible sports. Others are well known to certain groups of people, such as the vice president of University Relations, the director of Development, and the vice president of Public Affairs and Communication. To the students in a given dormitory, the rector is familiar. In departmental offices, there are always secretaries who interact regularly with faculty and students, and then there are the academic advisors.

A high percentage of those who work at Notre Dame, however, complete their tasks without a lot of fanfare and notice. Through the years I have come to appreciate the essential presence of those who perform behind the scenes and keep the daily, weekly, and monthly operations humming along while they are fully responsive to different circumstances and conditions.

Included in this category are those who plow the sidewalks and streets in the winter or keep the grass mowed when the campus is abloom. Others are involved with the power plant and basic maintenance, or the provision of food and catering. Every year, when the university is closed at Christmastime, fifty or sixty individuals come in to the Development Office to open mail and register year-end gifts to the university and then prepare responses to those who have been generous. These efforts take them away from their families as they work in otherwise empty office buildings.

Some jobs are simply 24-7, as we now say, by the nature of the work—particularly the police, security, infirmary, and fire safety operations as well as the telephone operators and those who attend to the needs of individuals who live on campus all year long, such as the head staff of the dorms and the residents of Corby Hall and the Presbytery. The university is also blessed with secretaries and office staff who process the paperwork and attend to the mail and the smooth flow of information. Other employees move furniture and deliver packages. The maids and janitors keep the living and work spaces clean and attractive. Those who work in the Morris Inn allow us to maintain our reputation as a center of warm hospitality.

Among those who work behind the scenes I have often been struck by those engaged in crowd control or the orderly flow of participants and spectators at sporting events, cultural activities, and occasions of worship. For example, a couple of ushers at every home football game oversee the two elevators in the renovated stadium. As far as I know, they never get to see the game itself. They welcome each group who uses the elevator and then thank them for coming and wish them a good day. The same is true of those at the Red Cross locations who attend to medical emergencies. Ticket takers and those who provide food are also essential to the smooth functioning of Notre Dame operations for the tens of thousands of visitors who come to the campus. And then there are those who clean up the common areas after the visitors have returned to their homes. Each succeeding day, Notre Dame makes a new start as if nothing disruptive had taken place, thanks to those behind the scenes.

SPORTS AND GAMES

Outdoor Basketball

Despite the fact that at Notre Dame snow often covers the ground for several months of the year, students and other members of our communities delight when the weather cooperates and they can enjoy the outdoors—thus, the long-established tradition of walking, jogging, and running around the lakes. The many athletic playing fields are in constant use during the fall and spring seasons. The proliferation of wooden benches throughout the campus allows people of every age to settle in and enjoy the beauty and wonder of a pleasant day. This is not to speak of lying on the grass with a group of friends, on a blanket or not, or sunbathing once the temperature rises above 50 degrees.

Among the structured outdoor locations, none is more popular than the various basketball courts. Bookstore Basketball celebrates the annual spring competitive tradition where the final games used to take place on the two courts immediately adjacent to the old bookstore, formerly called Badin Bog and now a green space immediately north of the Coleman-Morse Center. These two courts were inadequate in every way—with bent rims, warped backboards, an irregular surface, trees hanging over the edge of the court, and even an intrusive manhole cover. Yet during the era in which the bookstore courts were available, the players adjusted to the circumstances and somehow had fun. The event gained national recognition when featured one year in *Sports Illustrated.*

For many years the largest concentration of outdoor basketball courts was on the Stepan Center lot. Here, eight full-length courts were especially convenient when Flanner and Grace Halls housed undergraduate students. Because the Stepan courts also functioned as a parking lot during the day, it was important that they drain properly. As a result, playing on the court meant going uphill in one direction and downhill in the other. It also meant that the specified ten-foot height of the baskets was seldom realized. A further complication was that the Stepan courts were subject to crosswinds that could make a long-distance shot almost impossible. These courts, too, were plagued by minor problems—more warped backboards, irregular playing surfaces, and sometimes unswept sand. Once the bookstore courts were torn down, the championship games of Bookstore Basketball were held on the northeastern-most court and portable stands were erected, along with a table for media coverage.

In addition to the Bookstore and Stepan Center courts, for many years there were two full courts on the Lyons Hall parking lot. These courts, which still exist, were longer than regulation and involved somewhat of a trek to get from one end to the other. The biggest problem in playing basketball on the Lyons courts has been the prevailing wind off St. Mary's Lake. When a twenty- or thirty-mile-per-hour gale is blowing, only a layup or dunk suffices. This has meant that the Lyons games have tended to be more physical than the contests on the other two sites. Finally, there is the further problem of balls rolling into the road around the lakes.

There are two other locations where basketball courts have existed in my time at Notre Dame. The first was behind what was Holy Cross Hall. This court has been turned into a storage area for supplies for the Holy Cross community and for the Holy Cross priests who share an art studio in what used to be the gym of Holy Cross Hall when it was a seminary. The second was in the area adjacent to Carroll Hall on the path toward Fatima Retreat House. This single full court is still there but seems to get minimum use from the residents of Carroll Hall or from anyone else.

In the wake of the physical transformation of the campus, the university constructed two new courts just north of the Stepan courts and eight courts just west of the present bookstore. These ten sites were generally well received by the campus community. The surfaces are comparatively flat and well maintained, the backboards are straight and true, and there are no trees impeding the shooting lines. But in a well-intentioned effort to limit costs, the rims that were installed were double and exceedingly rigid when the balls hit them. As a result, outdoor games became more like bumper pool than like genuine basketball. As any basketball shooter can tell you, it is impossible to swish every shot, especially outdoors from long distances, so it becomes important for the rims to have an appropriate degree of give, a kind of shooters' roll. Without this, the only players who can score reliably are those close to the basket or those whose elevation enables them to shoot from above the rim.

Having discovered from many reports that only one more step remained for the new courts to serve us properly, I thought about conspiring with Coaches Mike Brey and Muffet McGraw to make the case. But then I thought, what the heck, so I got together with Jim Lyphout, our vice president of Business Operations, and he agreed to order replacement rims. Now, on all of our outdoor basketball courts, we have single breakaway rims that are state of the art. Let the contests begin.

Joggers and Runners

The majority of Notre Dame students come to us after having competed in athletics in high school. Overall, they have achieved a degree of balance between their academic commitments and their extracurricular activities. For some, physical exercise was just one more thing in the midst of a busy week. Others gained success in competition, even to the point of recognition at the city, state, or national level. Still others were recruited to play at the lower levels of NCAA competition but chose to come to Notre Dame instead. As a result, they need to make decisions about what form their athletic engagement will take and how much exercise they'll get in the course of a typical week.

Some compete as walk-ons in some of our Division 1A teams. Others become involved in club sports of one kind or another. A number participate in interhall athletics. Then there are those who work out or lift weights, or swim on a regular basis. All things being equal, I would describe the typical Notre Dame student as in shape and seeking physical exercise as part of a balanced and busy life.

The most common form of outdoor recreation seems to be jogging, running, and fast walking. The paths around the two lakes are favorite areas for those who like a soft surface and enjoy being in the company of nature. One can sit on one of the benches on Holy Cross Hill and watch a typical segment of the campus population move by on any given day when the weather is halfway decent. Some are outfitted in fancy sweat clothes, some wear earphones to listen to their favorite music, and then there are those who seem indifferent to how they look or what pace they keep.

When it comes to walking, it is more usual to see a couple of coeds making their way around the lakes or on some of the roads on campus rather than male undergraduates. The young women seem to be sharing their lives with each other and otherwise distracting themselves from any physical pain. In general, walkers seem to be less in a hurry to get the exercise over. A few carry small weights, which they swing effortlessly by their sides. The really slow walkers convey a sense of meditative reflection and the sheer enjoyment of the beauty of nature.

The joggers have a routine of running at the same time every day and along the same path. It is likely that they can tell you almost exactly how long their jog will take and how many calories they will use up in the process. It is common to see groups of men, as well as women, jogging together. Some are engaging in conversation and others are simply moving along in each other's company. Most of the jogging population are in reasonably good shape, but then there are those who may be keeping a New Year's resolution, responding to a charge from their physician, or trying to make up for excessive eating or drinking on the weekend. These joggers will often have a pained expression on their faces, and some huff and puff loud enough to be heard by people several yards away. It is probably best that they not stray too far from the beaten path lest they need the ministrations of the security police or an EMT.

Last, there are the runners, some so thin and effortless in their exercise that they were clearly experienced racers in high school. The fastest probably ran crosscountry before they came to Notre Dame. Some graceful runners resemble gazelles or pumas as they tear up the path, while others have a jerky gait that suggests that sometime in the future they might suffer from muscle and tendon problems. Groups of faculty, administrators, and staff run every day at the same time around the broad sweep of the campus. For them, regular running exercise is necessary for a healthy and happy life.

One sad segment of those who exercise outside on a regular basis are young women (and a few young men) who suffer from eating disorders. For them, physical exercise has become compulsive. It is the way that they respond to the fear that they are overweight and unattractive. I am no expert on such matters, but I have counseled enough students and read enough in the literature to know that it is hard to advise such individuals. At a minimum, they need to sort out the relationship between their exercise regimes and their self-image.

In my own life, I became a pretty regular jogger in my forties and fifties, especially in the summer and when the outdoor temperatures were moderate to hot. Then one day I decided that I didn't really like the jogging itself but only how I felt after it was over. That was when I started walking around the lakes and around the campus instead. Now I am more aware of my physical surroundings and allow myself more time for reflection and meditation.

During his time, one of the most famous joggers on campus was Father Mark Fitzgerald, C.S.C., who was a physical exercise fanatic up into his eighties. One of his favorite routes was around the old golf course. He often was dressed in disheveled clothes and looked like a refugee. Periodically, the security police would get a phone call about a possibly demented man who was seen jogging around the course. Right away they knew it had to be Father Fitzgerald. He died in his nineties, having done everything he could to cultivate a sound mind in a sound body.

Squirrel Joe

A certain undergraduate named Joe was spurned by a young lady in whom he had expressed a romantic interest. He was so angry that when he later saw a squirrel on the sidewalk, he was sure that it was laughing at him. Thus began an obsession with chasing squirrels that lasted for a couple of years. Once, when Joe was trying to catch a squirrel that had climbed an evergreen tree, a passerby yelled at him, "You can't chase that squirrel, it's cruelty to animals." Joe shouted back, "I paid twenty grand for the privilege of chasing this squirrel and chase it I will." His technique was to sneak up behind them and grab them between their front and hind legs so that they wouldn't bite.

The most exciting chase he ever participated in was behind the Sorin statue. It was springtime, and a large group of prospective students and visitors were being charmed by one of the campus tour guides. Joe charged through the crowd, climbed the maple tree behind the statue, and grabbed the critter. The tour guide went catatonic, and the group of prospective students and visitors milled about as Joe returned to the ground. Afterward, he phoned the RecSports office to inquire whether squirrel chasing could be declared a Junior Varsity sport, but they laughed at him and hung up. To this day, as far as I know, squirrel chasing has never been embraced by the broader university community. It seems that Squirrel Joe participated in a sport of one.

SQUIRREL JOE   87

Ushering at Notre Dame Stadium

The people who usher at Notre Dame Stadium perform a variety of tasks before, during, and after the football games. Some focus on crowd control or protect the field from intruders. Others work behind the scenes to run the elevators or check tickets or see to security. As a group, they are recognizable by their bright yellow jackets, and they warmly greet those who come to the games. In many ways they are agents of hospitality for the broader Notre Dame community.

Most of the ushers live in the general area of South Bend, but there are others who fly in from a long distance and make it a kind of vacation. Often the responsibility has been passed on from one generation to the next. They seem to love their work and the opportunity to be an integral member of the Notre Dame community, even if only for a few days of the year.

One usher told a story of serving on the visitors' side of the field. She met a member of the Rutgers University group who turned out to be the team chaplain and who had been a football historian for fifty years. It had always been his dream to visit Notre Dame and its stadium. He was totally in awe of the place. He noticed on her hat the gold pin of the Dome with an ND on it, and she finally gave it to him. He put it in his pocket, fully appreciative of the gift but not feeling free to wear it until after the game was over.

Another field usher recalled the first game in the aftermath of the terrorist attacks of September 11, 2001, in New York City. Some of the city's firemen had been invited on the field to watch the pre-game activities. All of them seemed to have a deep sadness in their eyes, as if they had witnessed hell on earth. When asked how big was the hole in the ground where the World towers had stood, one of the firefighters answered, "See this place? It's bigger than that." Another observed, "The thing I remember most was that when I came upon the rubble, the only thing that wasn't completely burned or pulverized was the soles of people's shoes. Just the bottoms of hundreds of people's shoes." A tall, athletic firefighter had his right arm in a cast. When asked if the injury was from that day, he replied, "Yes, but that is nothing. I'm the only one from my station who made it out alive. My brother-in-law and all my buddies who were in my wedding are gone." Still another firefighter remarked that after the attack, when someone put a long thermometer probe into the mass of rubble that was still too hot to remove, it measured 2100 degrees Fahrenheit.

Another usher, who has a couple of relatives who are women religious, was given a bottle of holy water to sprinkle on the Notre Dame players when they came out through the tunnel onto the field. She did so during a home game when the team beat Michigan, and the sister was convinced that her holy water had done the job. Then there is the story told by an usher about two sweet elderly women who, at halftime, pulled out a small paper sack of sandwiches. Each sandwich was made with blue and gold bread.

Women's Basketball Champions

Father Ted Hesburgh rightly identifies the two great structural changes that took place at the university during his term of distinguished leadership—the establishment of the predominantly lay Board of Trustees in 1967 and the decision to make Notre Dame coeducational on the undergraduate level in 1972. With regard to the latter, the university has made substantial progress over the years in trying to fully integrate women into the student body, the faculty, and the administration.

In 2001 the undergraduate student body elected their first female student body president. A number of women had served as vice president or in other major roles as class officers or the heads of various organizations, but it was an important transitional moment when Brooke Norton was elected. Again, in 2002, Notre Dame elected its second female student body president.

On the athletic front, Notre Dame women have won NCAA championships in fencing and in soccer and have been very competitive in many other intercollegiate sports. But the most highly visible symbol of success was the 2001 women's basketball team, which won the national championship dramatically in St. Louis against Purdue. Coach Muffet McGraw gradually built a competitive team and a substantial fan base as well. In the course of the 2000–2001 season there were several home sellouts, and the average attendance was the highest ever and one of the highest in the NCAA.

In what turned out to be a magical season, I had the good fortune to spend time with the coaches and the team in the locker rooms after major victories and in the final round of the NCAA tournament. What struck me was what a wonderful group of young women were representing the university. They were not only outstanding athletes but also articulate and full of humor. They had excellent rapport among themselves and were very generous in making themselves available to their growing group of fans, especially the younger ones. If ever there was a case of athletes being excellent role models for the next generation, the women's team surely qualified. Mark Bradford's book, *Nice Girls Finish First*, captured the essence of the season.

Three seniors—Ruth Riley, Niele Ivey, and Kelley Siemon—were leaders both on and off the court. Ruth accomplished the extraordinary feat of being Naismith Player of the Year, First Team All-American, and First Team Academic All-American. Her distinctive headband was imitated by young girls wherever she went. Niele, the point guard and the team dynamo, overcame two knee surgeries and suspicions that she would not be able to make it through the whole season. Kelley coped with a broken hand and continued to play in her characteristic slashing style, often employing an off-hand layup to break down the defense. The younger team members also made notable contributions. Alicia Ratay was the deadliest three-point shooter in the country. Ericka Haney was a tough defender who often scored by driving to the basket. In an age when coaches and players are frequently interviewed on television or by other media I have seldom seen a group as eloquent and reflective of the values of a university as Muffet and her players were. They combined self-confidence with humility, an awareness of the importance of the team with the recognition of individual contributions.

In St. Louis the semifinal game against Connecticut and the final game against Purdue were both nail-biters. In both games, the Notre Dame team fell behind and had to work its way back to victory. The tension in the stands (and beyond) was palpable. As a former Notre Dame basketball player and as someone schooled on the playgrounds of Washington, D.C., I have a pretty non-demonstrative style of spectating. It doesn't mean that I'm not intensely involved, but I learned long ago as an athlete not to show emotion, just to outperform your opponent. Nevertheless, at the end of the championship game in St. Louis I jumped over the barrier and ran onto the court. I even gave Coach McGraw a big hug on national television at mid-court. That's the joy of victory (and, thank God, not the agony of defeat). I can honestly say, having participated in sports championship seasons as a player, as a spectator, and as an administrator, the women's championship basketball season was the most fun of all.

Postgame Liturgies

One of the great traditions at Notre Dame is to accommodate the desire of many of the fans at home football games to participate in one of the campus Masses on Saturday late afternoon or evening immediately after a game. The overriding worry is that there will be no room in the desired place of worship. This is particularly true in the main body of the Basilica of the Sacred Heart as well as in its downstairs parish. We have to station a member of the security force outside the main entrance to the Basilica once it gets overcrowded in order not to violate the fire regulations.

Mass is available not only upstairs and downstairs at the Basilica but also at the Stepan Center and in many of the dorm chapels. People find out about these alternative locations either because a relative lives in the dorm or by word-of-mouth over the years. Congregations are stuffed into every possible nook and cranny. Many of the participants come as families, from toddlers to young kids, high-school students, current undergraduates, on up to parents and grandparents. No one seems to mind the crush, even in the un-airconditioned chapels when the weather is still warm. These Masses may not be elaborate in liturgical structure, but they are prime opportunities for worship.

The mood in the postgame chapels is obviously affected by the outcome of the game, but I have found that even when Notre Dame loses, everything is put into perspective when one attends Mass so soon after the contest is over. When collections are taken up for some charitable cause, such as the Center for the Homeless or one of the Holy Cross missions, people tend to be quite generous.

I like to celebrate these postgame dorm Masses, especially in Sorin Hall, because it gives me a chance to see former student friends of mine and their families. When I am not the celebrant, I usually hang out in my room so that people can drop by after the Mass is over. At one recent Mass in Sorin, the hall was packed to the rafters and I was in charge of the service. I asked a couple of volunteers to read and recruited a Eucharistic minister from the congregation. As I tried to maximize the number who could actually make it inside the chapel, I encouraged people to stand around the back along the wall. As it turned out, a young African American boy ended up in the presider's chair. When I finished the first part of the Mass and went to sit down for the readings, I found that my seat (and the only one available) was already occupied, so I decided to stand along the wall next to it. The cute youngster stared up at me in my liturgical gear as though I was a creature from outer space. I don't know what the people in the congregation thought, but there was no way I was going to take the boy's chair on the grounds of liturgical niceties.

One of the great signs of the influence that Notre Dame has had on its graduates is to see them coming back to Mass in the dorms with their own children. There is something so fundamental about common worship in the Notre Dame experience that our grads want to share it with the next generation. I hope and pray that one of the biggest problems on home football weekends will continue to be whether people can find a Mass where they can make it inside, no less find a seat.

A Hug for the Team Chaplain

It is customary for the team chaplain to bless the football players as they enter the locker room at the end of the game. As ten-point underdogs, Notre Dame had just scored an impressive win over a perennial rival in an early September game played in 88-degree weather at Notre Dame Stadium. One of the first players into the locker room was a smiling, three-hundred-pound, defensive lineman all sweated up with chalk and dirt covering his uniform. In his jubilation, he said, as he picked up the chaplain, "Thanks for the blessings, Father. What I really need is a hug."

SPECIAL DAYS
AND HOLY DAYS

Christmas on Campus

As one might expect at a Catholic university, the Christmas season at Notre Dame is celebrated in its own fashion by every subcommunity within the institution. Almost every large group in the workforce has its own time for festivity and sharing—even those functional units that host the parties for others, such as the Morris Inn and the dining halls. There is even a special celebration for those who work the night shift.

Student Government gives an award annually to the hall that has the best exterior decorations. This is a highly sought-after prize, and a lot of creativity and hard work go into lighting up the fronts of buildings and otherwise capturing a bit of the religious and secular aspects of the season. Those halls with porches, such as Sorin and Badin, usually take advantage of the roof of the porch to put up a three-dimensional display. Some of the older and more traditional dorms have a recognizable motif from year to year, such as lights outlining the ends of the building. Then there are those dorms that give awards for the best hall decoration and the best individual room display. For a couple of years, I was one of the judges in a women's dorm where a lot of money had been spent and hours employed in getting into the spirit of the season. It was, in fact, a daunting task to come up with only three winners after being overwhelmed by the number of participants in the contest.

Each year in the Rotunda of the Main Building, the university places an artificial tree that soars up two floors and is gaily decorated. In front of the tree, looking south, is a large crèche scene with many of the traditional Nativity figures. The oxen and sheep and other animals are large enough to attract instant attention from small children. Each year I sponsor a party for many members of the campus community who enjoy refreshments while the Bell Choir plays Christmas hymns, followed by the Glee Club. The sound resonates wonderfully in the Rotunda. In front of the Main Building, on the side by the Basilica, one of the fir trees is strung in lights and becomes a beautiful nighttime sight for those glancing up at the Dome from the south.

Perhaps the favorite Christmas locations for most of us, including the many visitors to the campus, are the Grotto and the Basilica of the Sacred Heart. The crèche scene at the Grotto is on the left looking toward Mary. The figures are almost lifesize, and a lot of care goes into constructing·a very moving image of the birth of the Lord. In the Basilica, in addition to the flowers, banners and streamers, and other colorful reminders of the season, there is a beautiful crèche scene in front of the Lady Chapel. This becomes, especially on Christmas Eve and on Christmas Day, a kind of pilgrimage place. There is something powerful and emotionally engaging about the contemplation of the mystery and wonder of Christmas. In the end, Christmas combines in these settings all of the simple joy and wonder of the children in our midst with the need for renewal and the celebration of one of the central mysteries of the Christian faith. There may be places in the world that do a better job of capturing the meaning of Christmas, but surely there is no institution that works harder at it than Notre Dame.

Holy Week at the Basilica

The basic structure of the Roman Catholic Mass is relatively simple. The first part usually begins with an introduction followed by an acknowledgment of one's sinfulness and an opening prayer. Then there are one or more readings taken from the Bible, followed by the Gospel and a homily. The second part of the Mass includes prayers for various intentions, the preparations of the gifts, a group of prayers before and after the consecration of the bread and wine into the body and blood of Jesus, and then the recitation of the Lord's Prayer. The last part includes Holy Communion, a final blessing, and the sending forth of the community to live that which they have celebrated in common.

It is possible to recite the words of the Mass, separate from the homily, in an unhurried fashion in about fifteen minutes, although many Eucharists go much longer, depending upon the number of hymns sung, the loquaciousness of the homilist, the elaborateness of the ritual, and the number of people participating. The typical weekday liturgy lasts about thirty minutes, and most Sunday Masses between forty-five minutes and an hour. Elaborate celebrations, such as the ordination of priests or bishops or the Holy Week Triduum, can go anywhere from one and one-half to two and one-half hours.

Catholics are sacramental people. They believe that the ordinary substances of everyday life can symbolize the presence of God—thus, the use of water, sacred oil, incense, and palm branches. Human artistic creativity can transform windows and walls and ceilings into visual conveyors of sacred history and the commemoration of holy men and women. When Catholics make the sign of the cross or pray before the tabernacle or make the Stations of the Cross, they are participating in a long ritual tradition. We do not pray to statues or pictures or crucifixes, but rather to those whom they represent. Mary, the mother of Jesus, is not literally our mother, but she has a special place in the Catholic firmament because of the role she played in the story of salvation. She mediates Christ's presence to us. The saints, the holy men and women who have gone before us in the community of faith, are heroic examples of

Christian faith lived to the full. Their stories can inspire us to follow their example.

As a Catholic university, Notre Dame is a heavily sacramental place. All of the major events in the school year include a large Mass, either in the Basilica or the Joyce Center or, sometimes, on one of the quads. Every dorm has its own chapel where Mass is regularly celebrated, and so do a number of the academic buildings. The Grotto is a popular site not only for personal prayer and reflection but also for Masses for dorm groups, undergraduate classes, alumni reunion classes, and retreat participants. But of all the sacred places on campus, the heart of our worship lies in Sacred Heart Basilica, both the campus-wide prayer place in the upper church and the Sacred Heart Parish in the crypt below. Sacred Heart Church was designated a basilica at the time of the celebration of the university's sesquicentennial in recognition of the central place that the church has and continues to play in the Notre Dame community. The heart of the Christian liturgical calendar is found during Holy Week, when we celebrate once again the passion, death, and resurrection of Jesus the Lord.

Passion (Palm) Sunday. By tradition the president of the university is the celebrant for the ten o'clock Mass at the Basilica on Passion Sunday. The ceremony begins on the steps of the Bond Hall, where the Gospel describing Jesus' triumphal entry into Jerusalem is read, palm branches are blessed, and the congregation walks with the members of the liturgical choir in procession through the main doors of the Basilica. I and the five or six concelebrants wear the red vestments specified for this day. Because this Mass is televised on cable every Sunday on the Hallmark Channel, there is an expectation that it will be completed in one hour. Not counting the fifteen minutes it takes to process from Bond Hall to the Basilica, it is still not possible to finish in the required time.

On this Sunday in 2004, the passion according to the Gospel of St. Luke was read in its entirety by a group of five of us. I took the part of Christ, as the celebrant usually does. Since I and many of the congregation had seen Mel Gibson's movie, *The Passion of the Christ,* fairly recently, it clearly affected my reading of the part as well as the sensitivity with which I listened to the rest of the text. The visual images of the movie were so powerful that it was almost impossible not to take them into account in responding to the passion story itself. In my short homily I tried to point to the relationship between Jesus' temptations in the desert before he began his public ministry (which revolved around the easy route to messiahship through the provision of food to the hungry masses, a powerful military force to carry the day against his enemies, and the use of miracles to win disciples through awe-inspiring deeds) and the picture of the Messiah as the suffering servant that was highlighted in the Gospel. In the Christian story there is no other way to the Resurrection except through the cross. During the course of the liturgy, I had a strong sense that the congregation had been affected by the movie in a way that was hard to pin down. They seemed fully motivated to give themselves over to a deep reflection on the significance of Holy Week and the difficult path that Jesus trod toward our salvation.

Holy Thursday. The Holy Thursday liturgy, which takes place at 5 p.m., was celebrated in 2004 by Father David Tyson, provincial for the Indiana Province of Holy Cross and former president of the University of Portland. The majority of the members of our local Holy Cross community concelebrated along with other priests who had come to the campus for Holy Week. John's Gospel was recited, and the focus was on Jesus washing the feet of his disciples at the Last Supper. Father Tyson spoke in his homily about a woman who had spent her whole adult life at Portland serving in the faculty–Holy Cross dining room and who was known for her upbeat spirit and the solicitous care with which she went about her work. He went on to reinforce the notion that true discipleship is well captured in the washing of feet, that is, in the ministry to God's people. Those of us who would be great in the kingdom need to be the servants of others. After the homily, Father Tyson proceeded to wash the feet of twelve members of the congregation who represented a broad cross-section of the university community.

One of the features of the Triduum and Holy Week is the presence on Thursday and Friday of those who will be baptized at the Easter Vigil on Saturday evening. As is specified in the liturgical rite, those who are to be baptized are dismissed right after the washing of the feet. All baptized members of the congregation stand with a hand raised in blessing over them before they depart. The catechumens will be welcomed to full membership during the Easter Vigil service itself. After the dismissal, and to the accompaniment of hymns, the holy oils are brought to a table in front of the main altar. After the distribution of Communion, the consecrated breads are carried in an elaborate procession with banners and incense from the main altar down the main aisle, then up the side, and back to the Lady Chapel. The hymn "Pange Lingua" is sung during the procession. The Lady Chapel, with its silver and gold reredos, is beautifully arrayed with flowers. When the service is over, the celebrant clacks a wooden mallet twice and the concelebrants and altar servers march off in silence. The Lady Chapel then becomes the altar of repose and the center of prayer throughout the evening. While it is not officially part of the Triduum, the office of Tenebrae is celebrated at 11 p.m. in the Basilica on Holy Thursday.

Good Friday. The Good Friday service, which is not officially a Mass but rather prayer and the distribution of Hosts consecrated on Holy Thursday, is focused on the veneration of the Holy Cross. In 2004, Holy Cross Father Nick Ayo, professor in the Program of Liberal Studies, was the main celebrant. The celebration began with the church in darkness and utter silence as the altar servers and the concelebrants made their way into the Basilica from the rear to a somber drumbeat from the choirloft above. After an opening prayer and two readings, the Passion according to the Gospel of John was sung. In his homily, Father Ayo focused not so much on who was responsible for the ignominious death of Jesus (theologically, we are all responsible), but rather on the underlying message that only the Easter mystery fully makes sense of both the necessity and the reality of his crucifixion.

After the homily, those to be baptized are once again dismissed. Nine prayers of intercession are said so that the saving power of Jesus' victory might be distributed across the whole human race. Then the celebrant moves down the main aisle from the rear of the church, chanting three times in progressively higher tones, "Behold the Wood of the Cross." Each time, more of the purple cloth covering the cross is taken off, to reveal a large cross about four feet high and two feet across. The celebrant reverences the cross with a kiss, and this devotion is in turn done by members of the congregation approaching concelebrants with smaller crosses throughout the church. Meanwhile, the choir sings the reproaches around the refrain, "My People, What Have I Done to You? How Have I Offended You? Answer Me." After everyone in the church has had a chance to venerate the cross, the celebrant stands before the main altar and turns in four directions while the choir and the congregation sing in Greek, Latin, French, Spanish, and English the refrain, "Holy God, Holy and Mighty One, Holy and Mortal One, Have Mercy On Us." After Communion, the congregation departs in silence with the empty tabernacle standing with its door open in the rear of the church at the Lady Chapel.

Easter Vigil. At the center of the concluding liturgy of the sacred Triduum during Holy Week is the celebration of the Easter Vigil.

Easter is the most important feast in the Christian calendar for it is at the heart of our faith and conviction. Jesus' resurrection from the dead is the source of our comfort and our hope.

Father Peter Rocca, C.S.C., the rector of the Basilica of the Sacred Heart, was the celebrant in 2004. His beautiful voice was put to full use, along with the liturgical choir, during the course of the two and one-half hour ceremony. The church was overflowing with worshipers, and there were about thirty concelebrants robed in white. At the beginning of the liturgy the church was dark, and the altar servers and concelebrants walked quietly forward to the altar. Then, using ancient symbols, there is a blessing of the new fire and the lighting of the Paschal Candle, which is carried in procession to the front of the church. Each member of the congregation has been given a candle, and these are all lit. Father Rocca sang the beautiful "Exsultet" from the pulpit. At this point the candles were extinguished, the church lights turned on, and the readings began. There were four readings from the Jewish scriptures, each followed by a hymn, then the singing of the "Gloria" followed by the Epistle and the Gospel. The homily was given by Father Bob Dowd, C.S.C., a faculty member in the Department of Political Science. He spoke of the source of our Easter joy, the reality of Jesus risen from the dead, and offered special words of welcome and encouragement to those about to be baptized. No one in the congregation knew that on that same morning his father had died after a long, debilitating illness. His words were even more telling in light of what he had been through himself in the last few days.

After the homily the rite of Christian initiation of adults took place for eleven new members of the Catholic community. Of the eleven to be baptized at the font in the entrance of the church, ten were students and one, Amy Tremel, was a longtime and very popular employee of the university. Each person individually, after responding to the questions, was baptized in water according to the Trinitarian formula. Their sponsors accompanied them throughout the ceremony and assisted them as they put on white robes to symbolize the purity of the life to which they were being called. After the baptism was completed, they were also confirmed. The rest of the Mass continued as usual, and at the time of Communion the newly baptized and newly confirmed also received their first Holy Communion. After the solemn blessing at the end, the Alleluias were sung and then the choir and congregation sang together the triumphant hymn "Jesus Christ Is Risen Today."

It should be noted that each day in the Triduum, additional services are held in the Basilica, including morning prayer and evening prayer and, on Good Friday, the Stations of the Cross. On Easter Sunday itself there are large crowds of worshipers in the upstairs Basilica and in the parish down below. And on Sunday night a student-oriented Easter liturgy is celebrated at 9 to an overflow crowd of well-dressed and enthusiastic young people who are proclaiming their faith in their home away from home.

There is no place else in the world that celebrates Holy Week and the sacred Triduum with more fervor, more conviction, or more preparation than at Notre Dame. People have been coming back to the campus for Holy Week for decades. Parents come because their children are singing in the choir or are involved in some other way in the services. Some attend because they know one of those to be baptized. Students have heard along the way that they should not graduate from Notre Dame without having participated at least one time in the Triduum.

For me, it is a kind of weeklong retreat. The liturgy is designed to engage all of the senses. The music is beautifully done by both the folk and liturgical choirs. There is, as well, the heavy use of incense, the streaming banners carried by the altar servers, the lighting of candles in sconces around the sides of the church, and the hearty participation by the congregation in every part of the liturgy. As someone who preaches at most of the public liturgies in which I participate, I delight in listening to the well-prepared homilies of my fellow Holy Cross priests. In this time when the American Church is preoccupied with the aftermath of scandal and misconduct, it is uplifting to worship with such a faith-filled congregation of people of every age, gender, race, and ethnicity. The liturgy helps us to express our aspiration that the Church will be a home for everyone.

Junior Parents Weekend

One of the great Notre Dame traditions, begun fifty years ago, is Junior Parents Weekend. Father Hesburgh, on the advice of his alumni director, decided to institute an event in February that would attract families to the campus and break up the monotony of the coldest and snowiest part of the school year. Like a lot of fine traditions, it started relatively small and took on a kind of trial-and-error resiliency. The dinner on Saturday night of the first weekend reportedly was held in the Morris Inn. A half-century later, the event barely fit into the hockey arena of the Joyce Center, with more than four thousand people present.

Junior Parents Weekend (JPW), as it has evolved, begins on Friday evening with a reception and dance in the Joyce Center. The basketball arena is set up with thematic booths and tables of hors d'oeuvres. Often some of the dining hall workers and student volunteers are dressed in period costumes, and sometimes bands or other ensembles provide background music. On these Friday evenings, I usually station myself somewhere in the line of passage in the basketball arena around 9 p.m. to greet people and pose for pictures until midnight, when the decorations come down to get ready for the next day. While it is a little awkward for some of the students who are showing off their parents to their peers, sometimes for the first time, the overall spirit is warm and family-oriented.

On Saturday morning, there are opportunities for the parents to meet teachers and to become familiar with some of the academic programs and opportunities at the university. Then on Saturday afternoon, each of the dorms hosts a lunch of sandwiches, chips, and potato salad or pasta for family members. Throughout the rest of the afternoon there are opportunities to tour the campus, meet other families, or participate in campus-based activities of the Junior Class. Then, in the late afternoon, a moving liturgy is celebrated in the basketball arena, followed by a festive dinner in the adjoining fieldhouse. The concluding event is brunch on Sunday morning, followed by a mad dash to the airport for the return home.

Each year confirms that we have found a format for an attractive and even inspiring celebration of the families who are part of our university community. It is a great example of role reversal when, probably for the first time in their lives, the students host their parents. In fact, the logistics for the weekend are generally handled by the students themselves with the assistance of a couple of staff from the Student Affairs Office. The planning effort goes on for months, everything from the menus for the meals to the type of music at the dances to the special events in the academic departments and in the dormitories. At the end of each JPW there is a thorough evaluation to determine where there is room for improvement. On the basis of this information, each new group has a chance to exercise its own creativity while following a well-established structural guide.

As many people have noticed, the vast majority of those who have moved to leadership positions for JPW have been women members of the Junior class—particularly the overall chairperson and those who are responsible for planning the Friday evening, Saturday evening, and Sunday morning events. One could speculate as to why women seem to gravitate to these jobs, but the end result is an outstanding success in service to the class and to their parents. One could even claim that JPW has become a great training ground for women prepared to run the world. I'd be willing to bet that these JPW planners have moved on to leadership in their professional lives and in the civic and not-for-profit organizations in which they participate after graduation.

Many parents have told me that their single most important experience at Notre Dame was Junior Parents Weekend, when we collectively say thanks to each of them for making a Notre Dame education possible for their daughter or son. It is a kind of relaxed warm-up for Commencement, without all of its pressures and rush. For fifty years now, Notre Dame has benefited from what started out as a way of breaking up the tedium and cold of February. It is a tradition that no longer needs any explanation other than that the families of the young people entrusted to our care fully deserve to be celebrated annually on our campus.

Universal Notre Dame Nights

The single most effective vehicle for outreach for the university's graduates and friends is the Alumni Association, with more than two hundred clubs spread throughout the country and world. Originally, the members of these clubs got together periodically for social and athletic events. More recently, they have supported continuing education efforts and provided opportunities for service by the club in their local communities. The local clubs vary in size, from around forty or fifty members to over one thousand. A large metropolitan area may have over ten clubs.

One of the traditions facilitated by the central staff of the Alumni Association is what was for many years called "Universal Notre Dame Nights," now "Notre Dame Celebrations"—events of varying degrees of elaborateness and cost, in which a representative from the campus, usually in the spring or summer, provides an update on university activities and events to the local clubs. There is a certain pecking order of preference by the clubs in terms of who their desired speaker might be. They can choose from several officers of the university, other administrators, selected faculty, and the athletic director and a few coaches. (Since the purpose is to highlight the non-sports side, Athletic Department participation is deliberately limited.) In a typical year, I usually take part in some ten Notre Dame Nights nationwide and up to five or six abroad. The turnouts are usually quite large, and I enjoy going to clubs of various sizes and in different geographical locations. The format of a typical Notre Dame Night includes greeting people at the door, some social time with drinks and appetizers, and a sit-down meal with speechmaking at the end and often the opportunity to take questions.

As I look back on over twenty years of participation in these events, either as a vice president or as president, my memories are generally quite positive. I have witnessed the great loyalty and love of the institution not only by its graduates but also by the so-called Subway Alumni, those who did not go to Notre Dame but ardently attend to its athletic fortunes. Depending on the time of year, prospective students and those already accepted for the incoming class are invited. On many occasions I have seen former students of mine or other people whom I have known for years.

Certain of these events stand out in my memory. For example, a Notre Dame Night in Charlottesville, Virginia, which is the home of the University of Virginia, took place in a church basement and the meal was a potluck supper. Nearly all of the people present were graduate students at the University of Virginia, with limited resources for a fancy sit-down dinner. The spirit of the evening was great, and it reminded me of our family picnics when I was growing up.

The smallest group that I ever visited was in Calgary, in Alberta, Canada. In that area we have only five graduates of the university, four of whom are former hockey players.

The meal itself was in someone's home around the dinner table. Afterward, we had a reception elsewhere, to which the alumni had invited some of their friends to hear a report on a summer service project that the club was sponsoring to work with teenage prostitutes.

On two occasions, when still a vice president, I gave my talk in a hotel where the ballroom was partitioned off and where next door to our dinner was either a band or a revival meeting. One event was a wedding reception where the noise carried over and made it almost impossible for anyone to hear what I had to say. The other was a Christian revival group with a rather noisy preacher and a congregation shouting out "Amen" and "Alleluia." At the beginning of my talk I urged my listeners to prove that we could be just as fervent in our "Amen" shouting as the people next door.

When I first started going to Notre Dame Nights, it was still common in the question-and-answer period that followed the after-dinner speech for old graduates to ask about coeducation. Implied in these questions was that the change from the traditional single-sex university had been a big mistake. But it wasn't long before the male graduates of the past were sending their own daughters and granddaughters to Notre Dame. All of a sudden, their pride in the achievements of their own family members far exceeded any concern about the break with history.

One thing that I have learned from getting around to most of the clubs through the years is how fortunate we are to have such strong leadership at the local level. To run a vibrant and active club is very demanding for already busy people. It is out of love for the university and a desire to make a difference that club presidents and other officers are willing to devote the time and energy to making the local club thrive. And, of course, Chuck Lennon and his staff in the Alumni Association do a great job in fostering a loyal spirit among the club leaders and among those elected to the Alumni Board.

Some clubs prefer to invite guests to the campus for a Mass and Communion breakfast, a send-off ceremony for incoming students, a golf tournament, or some other special event. However, our biggest change from the regular format was when we kicked off our fund-raising endeavors through the use of satellite technology to introduce the campaign from the campus to the various local clubs. This allowed us to have a fair level of immediacy while still staging a major event on campus.

While the logistical challenges of organizing Notre Dame Nights for all the clubs in a given year are daunting, I personally have been forced to miss a scheduled evening only two or three times, always on the basis of terrible weather in the area. As far as I know, the event has gone on, even in the absence of the scheduled speaker. Probably the best way for me to describe the Universal Notre Dame Night phenomenon is that it is a kind of institutional family reunion. The challenge is to make it convenient, attractive, and affordable as well as interesting to a broad cross-section of graduates. Like all family reunions, it is worth having, even if not everyone shows up. But the very best of these events are well attended, fun to be a part of, and a great affirmation of our common identity.

Commencement Weekend

Commencement weekend at Notre Dame is a time of pomp and circumstance as well as great joy and celebration. It brings together families from across the country and around the world to participate in a dramatic moment of transition in the lives of our graduates. For the faculty, staff, and administration of the university, Commencement weekend is a time of transition coupled with a feeling of completion. By then, grades have been turned in, courses completed, bills paid, and everything done to complete the academic year with style, dignity, and fun.

As is the case for other great, well-attended events at the university, a planning group meets throughout the year. Its members build upon the evaluation of the successes and failures of the previous year, tweaking the Commencement routine if necessary. These weekends resemble each other in structure and form, yet each year's events are unique in their own way and at least partly reflect the mood of the campus, the state of the nation and world, and uncontrollable factors such as the weather.

The first guests from out of town begin to arrive on Thursday. The first formal event of the weekend, "The Last Visit to the Basilica of the Sacred Heart and the Grotto," takes place on Thursday evening. Through the years this has grown as an attraction, and the Basilica is filled with a mix of students, parents, and family members as well as a few rectors and faculty. The service combines scripture readings, hymns, and reflections, and the Senior Class Fellow gives a brief address. But the highlight is a kind of reprise of the last four years from the point of view of four undergraduates, who try to capture some of the events of their time at Notre Dame, combining nostalgic reminiscences with humorous asides. I and a couple of other Holy Cross administrators sit in the sanctuary and preside over the ceremony, but we have a limited role.

At the completion of the prayer service in the Basilica, the assembled congregation makes their way toward the Grotto, picking up lighted candles as they go. They are greeted with a few songs by the Glee Club, and then there are a series of reflections by the university president, the executive vice president, and vice president of Student Affairs. The leader of the Senior Class accepts a lighted candle, which is then placed in the interior of the Grotto as a symbol of the class as a whole. After the final blessing, the Alma Mater is sung and the sign of peace is exchanged across the courtyard. This is an especially impressive moment for the parents and family members because it captures what passing on the faith to the next generation is all about.

Friday of Commencement week is full of smaller-scale events that are organized by different academic units, the residence halls, and some of the student activity groups. On Friday evening, there is a band concert on the lawn between Walsh Hall and LaFortune Student Center. My duties on Friday night include attending an awards dinner for graduate students honored for their academics and leadership. Afterward there is an open reception for all graduate students receiving degrees and their families in the McKenna Hall atrium. I try to greet as many of them as I can and wish them well as they move on to employment either in the academy, corporate life, or some other area. Many of these graduates are from other parts of the world, and it is obvious that they have very much enjoyed their experience at Notre Dame and are somewhat reluctant to leave our campus.

On Saturday the pace picks up considerably. In the morning there are the ceremonies commissioning new members of the military graduating from our ROTC contingents. The members of Phi Beta Kappa are installed. Meanwhile, I am engaged in Washington Hall for the so-called Sending Ceremony for approximately 180 members of the Senior Class who are going to give a year or more of service after graduation. They are involved in everything from Holy Cross Associates to the Alliance for Catholic Education, the Peace Corps, and many specific projects sponsored by Catholic dioceses or religious communities. I speak at this event, trying to offer encouragement and reinforcement to parents who may have a certain anxiety about whether a year or more of service is good for their daughter or son and about having their offspring go another year without a source of income. The main speaker for the morning is usually a former post-graduation volunteer or, in some cases, a couple, who reflect on their experience with all of its challenges and rewards. Some of these individuals have stayed in the nonprofit world and others have moved on to conventional careers, but their lives have been influenced and changed by the risk that they took in participating in one of these post-baccalaureate programs of service.

On Saturday afternoon some of the halls will hold lunches and some of the academic units will have special ceremonies for their graduates-to-be. In the mid-afternoon I proceed to the Eck Center to meet informally with graduates and their families and to pose for a few pictures as well. A reception follows for international student graduates and their families, who represent a broad cross-section of the world as well as the international character of Notre Dame.

The highlight of the whole weekend for me is the Baccalaureate Mass held in the basketball arena of the Joyce Center late Saturday afternoon. One of the marvelous things about Notre Dame is that we have the same number of people for the Mass as we do for the Commencement exercises the next day. It is my privilege, along with many priest concelebrants, the local ordinary, and other episcopal guests, to preside at the liturgy and to preach. Music is provided by the combination of choirs as well as by members of the Notre Dame concert band. The graduates in caps and gowns sit together, apart from their families. Amazingly, during the Mass we are able to distribute the Hosts to 13,000 communicants in twenty minutes. After Communion there is a ceremony in which I bless a large American flag, donated by the Senior Class, which will fly over the campus from the flagpole in the South Quad in the coming year.

After the completion of the Mass, it has been my custom in recent years to take a slow and leisurely walk over to the area by the reflecting pool in front of the Hesburgh Library. Since there is about an hour before I host the dinner on the top floor of the library for honorary degree recipients and other university guests, officers, and trustees, I usually pose for a few pictures with graduates who are wandering that way and then simply sit on a bench and take it all in. The dinner is primarily a social event with little speechmaking, a special occasion to offer hospitality to our guests. We usually offer around ten honorary degrees each year. We believe that a cohort of degree recipients enhances the value of each honorary degree more than would be the case if we only honored one person at a time.

Sunday for me is like a blur as we conclude Commencement weekend. I begin my morning by preaching at a prayer service held by the Notre Dame Law School in the Basilica of the Sacred Heart as one of their three ceremonies on the same day for graduates and friends. After preaching early in the service, I excuse myself and take a bit of a break. Next is the university-sponsored luncheon in the Monogram Room in the Joyce Center for honorary degree recipients, the Laetare Medalist(s), the trustees and officers of the university, and other guests. We usually invite any faculty and staff who have a son or daughter graduating to join us. We also give special recognition to the student with the highest average in each of our undergraduate degree programs as well as to the officers of the student body and Senior Class. Meanwhile, in other parts of the campus there are ceremonies with individual recognition to personalize the weekend for the families. There are also various venues where one can eat lunch and otherwise recapture one's energy in the midst of a busy weekend.

Finally, we come to the main event. The Commencement exercises are held in the Joyce Center arena from about 2 to 4 p.m. The platform party marches out promptly to the strains of ceremonial music proper for the occasion. Faculty members in their academic robes lead the procession, with one of their number carrying the university's ceremonial mace. The provost serves as emcee and introduces each of the separate sections of the ceremonies. First, a student selected from among the candidates for valedictorian says the opening prayer. The valedictorian speaks to the assembly on behalf of the student body, followed by the awarding of honorary degrees and the Commencement address. The provost then acknowledges students and faculty who have received special recognition during the course of the year. The awarding of the Laetare Medal brings a brief response from the recipient(s). The second half of the program is taken up with the granting of degrees, starting with those who receive the Ph.D., who come forward with their dissertation director one by one. All other degrees are granted in groups, ending with baccalaureate candidates, who are introduced by their respective deans.

Our graduation ceremony is a classy, tradition-laden affair. Generally, the students and their families are respectful of the various speakers. In the late 1970s and early 1980s there were more high jinks than there are now. On occasion, a group of students or faculty might protest a Commencement speaker or an invited guest, but those objections have been civil in style and tone and nothing like what some other campuses have experienced. Over the years we have had heads of state, especially presidents of the United States. My last event, other than posing for pictures with my gown, cap, and medal, is to make a brief appearance at the Law School ceremonies, this time in front of the reflecting pool of the Hesburgh Library. Then I can call it a day—a very special day.

MEMORABLE
INDIVIDUALS

Reverend Theodore M. Hesburgh, C.S.C.

At the time of his retirement in 1987, Father Ted had served for thirty-five years as the fifteenth president of the University of Notre Dame. Considered by many to be one of the great academic and civic leaders of the second half of the twentieth century, he has also been an influential figure in American Catholic Church history. Born in Syracuse, New York, he joined the Holy Cross Seminary program at Notre Dame and proceeded through its various stages toward ordination. He did much of his theological training in Rome, where he learned to function in Latin as well as in Italian and French. He returned to the United States to Catholic University to complete his doctorate in theology, his dissertation focusing on the role of the laity in the Church.

His first assignment after ordination and graduate work was to the University of Notre Dame, where he first taught theology, served as pastor to the University Village married students who had returned from military service in World War II, and lived in Farley Hall. In those early days his ministerial engagements were similar to most of his Holy Cross confreres, at a time when one was expected to participate in many tasks simultaneously with as much skill as one could muster.

Having recognized the young priest's administrative potential, John Cavanaugh, the fourteenth president of Notre Dame, invited him to serve as executive vice president. This provided an opportunity for Ted to become familiar with budgetary, fund-raising, academic, athletic, student-life, and other facets of the university. At that time, because the president of the university was also the local religious superior (a canonical position), the term of service was limited to six years. Thus, in 1952, Ted Hesburgh succeeded John Cavanaugh as president. It is noteworthy that he invited Ned Joyce to become his executive vice president. Their collaboration would last thirty-five years.

Father Ted, as he is known by most of his friends, has always been a handsome man with piercing eyes and boundless energy. From his own report, he was never much of an athlete and has never had any particular regimen of exercise. Rather traditional in religious practice, his inclinations have been toward progressive ideas when it comes to theology, Church structure, and political reform. Ideas and theoretical discussions that have practical results for those without rank or status in society have always attracted him. He might be best described as open-minded but not faddish; he has the attitude that if he can't understand an issue or problem, it has been poorly explained rather than being beyond his comprehension.

In the course of his work he has traveled widely within the United States and throughout the world. By the time of his retirement he could claim to have been in at least ninety countries and was intent on seeing as many more as he could in his lifetime. He has been blessed with the stamina and strong stomach of the dedicated traveler and is always interested in the wonders of new places and unknown peoples. Some of his traveling has been done with trusted companions on a regular basis, such as Christmas vacations with C. R. Smith, the former CEO of American Airlines, and Holy Cross Provincial Howard J. Kenna, his good friend. Ted has always been sensitive to the special customs and traditions of the places he has visited and can describe them in vivid detail. His linguistic training while studying in Rome has given him the confidence to learn new languages. Spanish and Italian are probably his best, but he can get by in French and German and knows smatterings of Portuguese, Mandarin Chinese, Arabic, and Japanese.

The best and most accurate description of Father Ted is that first of all he is a priest. He speaks often about his vocational calling and about the great joy that his priestly ministry has given him through the years. Having worn many hats in university administration and in service on not-for-profit and governmental boards, he always dons his clerical dress in formal situations and introduces himself as Father Ted, his first and truest identity.

Ted has expressed his openness to broadening the eligibility for admission to the Roman Catholic priesthood, but never out of a desire to change his own circumstances. His rationale for such a move, if it ever happened, would be the needs of the Church and not the personal needs of those who have felt excluded by its policies. Ted often refers to the number of famous people who have turned to him for priestly counsel, whether they happened to be Catholic or not. He is of the opinion that being a priest in circles where the presence of priests is unusual has given him a unique opportunity to minister to those outside the fold.

One revealing dimension of Ted as priest is his commitment to the daily celebration of the Eucharist. Except in times of sickness, he has celebrated the Eucharist every day of his priestly life. For Ted this devotion is not a function of guilt or legal obligation but rather an experiential recognition that the reception of the body and blood of the Lord is his prime source of spiritual nourishment. Like many priests in the modern era, Ted has celebrated Mass not only in conventional places such as churches and chapels but also onboard ship, in airports, in hotel rooms, and wherever human beings might be found.

On his travels, Ted has always carried a large briefcase that holds vestments, sacred vessels, and other essentials for the celebration of Mass. In most situations, a congregation, even if small, has been readily at hand, but if not, Ted has invited his traveling companions, fellow hotel guests, or startled passersby to join him for the Eucharist. Some of these occasions have included people who were Jews, Muslims, Hindus, Buddhists, or nonbelievers as well as members of other Christian denominations. They would feel honored to attend, even if they weren't familiar with the basic elements of the ritual, which Ted will often explain in his homily. In the years after his retirement, in his office on the top floor of the library, he has frequently sought out someone to join him for Mass from among the undergraduate and graduate students working in their carrels.

When it comes to relaxation, nothing has given Ted more enjoyment than spending time at the university property at Land O'Lakes, Wisconsin, where he enjoys staying in a small cabin and going fishing with one of the staff members. These trips have given him the opportunity to read, which, until experiencing major eye problems, he had done voraciously, while decompressing from the year ending and preparing for the next one. In a sense, Ted is an outdoorsman, although not an avid hunter or bird-watcher. The contrast between his usual duties and the natural beauty of the almost twenty lakes on the Land O'Lakes property has been a source of joy and reenergizing for him.

Ted, as noted, was an inveterate reader until the onset of macular degeneration. In the course of years, some of his reading matter was job-related, such as analyses of trends in higher education or the burst of publications in the wake of Vatican II on matters theological and ecclesiological. He is also intrigued by science and its impact on human well-being. Ted also worked his way through the illuminating reports generated by the staff of the various commissions and committees that he has served on or chaired. For him, reading was the primary way of remaining a lifelong learner. He has a particular love of history and biography with their studies of leadership, and he has a special interest in the Civil War and the Second World War. He reads fiction sparingly, usually books recommended to him by others. Even after the loss of most of his eyesight, his education continues with taped books supplied by the Library of Congress.

Ted has always been a welcomed public speaker, especially beyond the campus. On campus, he has developed the habit through the years of distracting attention from on-campus controversies by talking about his outside activities, leading to a gentle chide about being not only a name-dropper but also a country-dropper. However, Ted can speak and preach insightfully to crowds large and small about fundamentals such as life and love and human happiness. His funeral homilies, especially for people whom he had known well, set a perfect tone, combining a faith perspective with a deft summary of the deceased person's finest characteristics and achievements.

His best public presentations through the years have contained interesting stories and anecdotes. Indeed, in his later years, Ted has become known as an accomplished storyteller. His memory for times and places and significant details, often years and decades after the event, remains extraordinary. His autobiography, *God, Country, Notre Dame*, was on the *New York Times* best-seller list. Because he has often been in the company of popes and presidents, titans of industry, famous media figures, and people in the entertainment field, his audiences usually have felt that they are accompanying him on his journeys. His last book, *Travels with Ted and Ned*, is really a collection of stories about people whom Ted and Ned Joyce encountered on their post-retirement trips.

Ted has a special affinity with the military, especially the United States Navy. He served for a period of time on the Board of Visitors at the Naval Academy in Annapolis, and the continuing football rivalry between Notre Dame and Navy is a source of pleasure for him. He knows that the presence on campus of the Navy training programs during the Second World War saved the university from possible bankruptcy. While an advocate for peace and a visionary in its structural implementation, Ted has always accepted the necessity for countries to have military forces in a sometimes dangerous world. This has also meant that the ROTC programs have been welcomed on the campus, even in the midst of the social turbulence during the Vietnam War.

Always proud to be a member of the Congregation of Holy Cross, Ted is happy to explain what the C.S.C. (Congregatio a Sancta Croce) means after his name and how it works in Latin but not in English. During his years as president he was elected as delegate to every Provincial Chapter and to all of the General Chapters as well. These meetings usually went on for a couple of weeks and took him away from his usual routines, but he saw them as necessary participation in the governing structures of his religious community. Ted is invariably happy to do what he can to assist the institutions run by the Holy Cross priests, brothers, and sisters whether in this country or around the world. His presence at an event often generates additional income for the institution or activity.

It goes without saying that Ted is a unique combination of thinker, activist, and fund-raiser. He has understood well that people give money to institutions that they believe in and that such institutions are created and developed on the basis of compelling ideas and visions. When he took over as president, the University of Notre Dame had no tradition of successful fund-raising and had a minuscule endowment. He knew early on that the best universities were generally those that had the highest endowment. He recognized at the same time that Notre Dame was resource-poor in terms of facilities, faculty and staff salaries, and financial support for students at all levels. As president he oversaw the first systematic fund-raising efforts in the university's history and became the primary spokesman for its goals, with the result that the university excelled in one development campaign after another. When Father Ted finally stepped down as president after thirty-five fruitful years, Notre Dame had begun to emerge as the leading Catholic university in the country and the world. This is the legacy that he has passed on to the next generation.

Paul Fenlon

Paul Fenlon lived for over sixty years in Sorin Hall, where I currently reside. He was a professor of English and, after having taught many generations of Notre Dame students, effectively retired at Sorin. On home football weekends more than one generation of the same family would stop by to say hello. He always dressed nattily and had a kind of dignity and aplomb about him that won the respect and attention of others. He never married and was one of the last of the great Notre Dame "bachelor dons," that is, unmarried male professors who chose to live with and among the students.

I first moved into Sorin Hall in the 1978–79 academic year. Father Dave Porterfield, C.S.C., the rector at the time, asked me if I would take the second-floor turret room above Professor Fenlon. It seemed that the aging don was being disturbed by the students above him who bounced basketballs and made other noise. I readily agreed. Then, after I had lived in Sorin for awhile, I had the opportunity to visit Professor Fenlon's room on the first floor. It was like walking into the setting of a Victorian novel; nothing had been disturbed for years. He was an inveterate smoker, and there were full ashtrays all over the room. In fact, there was no furniture or accessory in his room that conveyed a sense of modernity or stylistic interest. I thought at the time, and I still do, that the room captured the spirit of the man.

In one of my first years in the dorm there was a group of students whom Professor Fenlon had befriended and who were often found in his company. He had helped one of them complete a senior thesis, a history of Sorin Hall from the beginning to the present, and they, in turn, helped to solve a university problem. Those responsible for the maintenance and well-being of the dorms had decided that Professor Fenlon's room needed to be replastered and repainted, but he kept resisting their overtures and the renovators were stymied. His student friends came up with the idea of taking advantage of his absence during his annual two-week vacation to visit his relatives in the East. The students took photographs of the room from every possible angle. Then, when Professor Fenlon went on vacation, the university took out everything, plastered and painted, and then returned all the furnishings to approximately where they had been when he left—including the full ashtrays. Professor Fenlon returned from his vacation, and since he made no complaints or indicated that anything was awry, everyone presumed that the surreptitious plan had worked. I have my doubts. I think he was simply too humble to say anything after the fact. In any case, it was the only clandestine renovation of a university room that I am familiar with.

One summer in late August, when the only residents of the dorm were myself, Professor Fenlon, and a group of visitors left over from a university conference, there was a tornado alert. I rushed around the dorm with my scanner radio so that I could listen to the weather reports while we fled to the most protected part of the building. I can't say that I felt completely safe, but the reports on the radio indicated that, although tornadoes had been spotted in several places in the area, none was headed for Notre Dame. The five or six campus visitors staying in the dorm were manifestly nervous. Professor Fenlon, on the other hand, was not prone to let his routine be interrupted. He wanted to get out on the porch where he could see what was going on. I explained to him that this would be unsafe, and he reluctantly accepted my opinion on the matter. When the all-clear was sounded, we went back to our respective rooms. If I had not been around, I suspect that Professor Fenlon would have toughed it out in his room, oblivious to any danger. After surviving sixty years in a student dormitory, he was not likely to be afraid of a tornado or two.

As his physical and mental condition declined, Professor Fenlon was allowed to move into the infirmary. As much as possible he tried to take periodic walks back to Sorin Hall to say hello to people. I knew his condition had taken a turn for the worse when this picture of propriety, who had always called me "Father" even after living as neighbors for years, began to address me as "big fellow." The first time he said it I almost chuckled, but I came to realize that he was losing his sense of reality.

When Professor Fenlon finally died, a large contingent of students came to his funeral. He was the last and perhaps the greatest of a special breed. He survived all the transitions in student life over sixty years, not the least of which was the amplification of sound. He personified that integration of learning and life that is found in profound philosophers. He was a man of dignity and charm and faith, and several generations of Notre Dame students were the beneficiaries of his loving and tender presence. Professor Fenlon is memorialized in a Sorin Hall plaque.

Emil T. Hofman

He was probably the best-known professor of the 1970s and 1980s. His Friday chemistry quizzes were legendary. During his term as director of what was then called the Freshman Year of Studies, he counseled several generations of Notre Dame students. He was always a participant in local alumni events around the country and likely possesses the most extensive video collection of Notre Dame events in existence. He is, of course, Professor Emil T. Hofman. In fact, he was my own professor in chemistry lab.

Now, Emil has found his own distinctive mode of living out his well-deserved retirement. He walks with the help of a cane, but otherwise he seems full of life and energy. Each weekday he arrives in time for the 11:30 a.m. Mass in Sacred Heart Basilica. He always sits about one-third of the way back on the righthand side of the transept looking at the altar. Immediately following Mass, he makes his way to a bench on the path directly between the Main Building and LaFortune Student Center. Emil stays there for hours at a time, dressed for the weather, engaging in his own reflections and chatting with passersby, only the older of whom appreciate his legendary status at the university. Some sit and chat for awhile, others walk on with a hearty hello. This man who was so busy for so long with his academic responsibilities and his administrative tasks now can focus on the one constant that brings him delight. He has become Notre Dame's greeter extraordinaire.

One can only speculate about what goes through Emil's mind as he spends quality time in this often quiet setting surrounded by the lush beauty of nature. Surely he knows the satisfaction of a job well done. May we all hope and pray that when the rush of our active life has slowed, we, too, might find a bench in the midst of the campus to commune with God and to let the past, present, and future flow into one.

Father Duck:
Charles Doremus, C.S.C.

By the time I joined the Holy Cross community at Notre Dame, Father Charles Doremus was long retired from his ministry on campus. In his retirement he had become identified with his daily practice of walking around the lakes and feeding the ducks. Day in and day out, even in the midst of the snow and freezing winds of winter, Father Doremus fed the waterfowl along the two lakes. And in line with the propensity of Notre Dame people to connect individuals with the work they do, Father Doremus began to be called, affectionately, "Father Duck."

However, as I discovered after a number of years, there was another side to this story of befriending wildlife. It turned out that Father Doremus was also a bit of a Darwinian in his perspective on nature. It seems that every spring, having established a close rapport with the ducks, he would decide which among them had reached a point where they could contribute in another way to humanity.

Early in the morning before most other people were up, he would bring a burlap bag to the lake and cull out two or three of the ducks that had ceased to be the objects of his affection and attention. He would grab them and bring them back to his room in Corby Hall. There they would be dispatched, de-feathered, and otherwise prepared for roasting. Then he would invite some of his friends to a grand banquet where the main course was filet of duck. Whether his guests ever drew the connection between the ducks on the lake and the ducks on their plates was never noted. While I was both too young and too naive ever to be invited to one of these meals, I have heard that a fine time was had by all.

Father Doremus eventually died, and I was one of the concelebrants at his funeral. As is our tradition in the Holy Cross community, we lined up two-by-two in front of the casket on its way to the Holy Cross Cemetery on the road to St. Mary's College. As we walked down the hill from the church past the Grotto and took a left on St. Mary's Road, I wondered whether the ducks recognized the significance of this moment. Soon after, I saw that the ducks that were sitting quietly by the side of the lake suddenly stirred and started to accompany the funeral procession toward the cemetery. Maybe it was just my imagination, but I thought I heard them quacking something on the order of "Good-bye, Father Duck, and Godspeed. Thanks for the food. But no thanks for the price that some of us had to pay to get it."

Brother Boniface
Landenberger, C.S.C.

Brother Bonny, as he was known by successive generations of students, worked at Notre Dame for thirty-four straight years. He had been born in Germany and, after serving in the German army in World War II, came to the United States, joined the Congregation of Holy Cross, and was asked to be the sacristan at Sacred Heart Church. Through most of his early years, when members of the local religious community celebrated daily private Masses on the altars in the basement of the church, Brother Bonny had to be ready for the first group at 5:30 a.m. This meant that he had to prepare each of the altars three different times, assign servers, and put out the vestments. After the morning Masses were over, he had to clean up everything.

Brother Bonny's duties included cleaning the lower and upper parts of the church each day. He derived his greatest sense of satisfaction in the work to beautify the Grotto. He also baked the Eucharistic bread and fermented the wine for Mass from grapes grown at St. Joseph's Farm, which was run by the Holy Cross brothers. Given the responsibility of shopping on behalf of the local Holy Cross community in South Bend, he would go to town on the streetcar and pick up prescriptions for the infirmary as well as deposit the Sunday collection in the bank, which he did by discreetly carrying the money in a roll of newspapers.

I remember Bonny in the later stages of his apostolic life at Notre Dame as kind-hearted, friendly, and efficient. On a number of occasions when I was a student, he recruited me out of the congregation to help serve Mass. He was not only a hardworking individual but also often the public face of the university and the community. His life is a fitting reminder that even the sacred side of our life as a worshipping community requires constant time and attention.

Student-Friendly Professors

In all of the university's printed and video material we espouse the highest possible commitment to learning for its own sake and for preparation for a life of service. This presumes that students will be highly motivated in their academic endeavors and lead rich, well-balanced lives. Nevertheless, the frailties of human nature sometimes intrude into the realities of everyday life on campus, especially among undergraduate students.

As a result, certain professors have stood out in the consciousness of their students as reliable guarantors of a high grade-point average. In the dormitories and in other undergraduate networks, the word passes from one generation to the next. Take Professor X's course because he/she gives a relatively light workload and generous marks. It could be that this professor is also an excellent pedagogue and a great inspiration in every way. But given the choice between an assured grade and an inspiring teacher, sometimes students will choose the former.

In my time as a student, three professors in particular—all dedicated to their students and intent on providing a good educational experience—had garnered reputations as easy markers. One was Jake Kline, a longtime Notre Dame baseball coach who also taught math, especially introductory courses to first-year students. Those were the days of the six-point grade system in which it was extremely difficult to earn a six or even a five in any course. Jake was a wonderful man whom I came to know rather well after my student days were over. His nickname was "99 Kline," and he was reputed to have said that he would never keep anyone away from the playing field or the altar, meaning that he had a special mission to keep athletes and seminarians eligible. I must confess that I chose Professor Kline and attribute to him all of my success in completing my undergraduate math requirement.

Another well-known easy marker was Father Thomas Brennan, C.S.C., whose nickname was "88 Brennan." He sometimes taught courses where 70 to 80 percent of the class was student-athletes, often from the most celebrated teams. Father Brennan was quite an athlete himself and was known to have the best bowling average when the bowling alleys were situated beneath the old bookstore; he was also said to be unbeatable as a handball player. If one of Father Brennan's students was seen nodding off or on the verge of indifference, he would hurl a chalk eraser at him. He was also known to toss books of matches, which some offenders were able to snatch deftly out of the air.

The third professor was Father Ed Murray, C.S.C., who had the reputation of having given more fives and sixes in the six-point system than any other professor at Notre Dame. He taught courses in the Irish exodus and Irish history, and many students who had only a dim acquaintance with anything related to Ireland would show up in his class. He had a habit of posting his final grades outside his room with ID numbers and without names. One time, when I was a student, just to confirm his reputation, I went by to check the list. Everything that had been said about his courses was true. I had never seen such high grades for any class that I had ever taken at Notre Dame.

It is fair to say that every generation has had its professors who were highly sought after for reasons that had little to do with the content of their courses. Certainly, it is a sacred prerogative of each professor to decide what grades should be given. Some teachers, particularly in science and engineering, are prone to employ a bell curve so that there is some kind of uniform distribution of grades. It is also the case that the average grades at Notre Dame have gone up over time, a fact at least partially attributable to the high quality of the student body. Indeed, all of the so-called prestige universities, both public and private, now assign higher grade-point averages in general than they did a decade or two ago. Thus, the search for the easy-marking professor may not be as high on the agenda for students today as it was in my era.

There was one occasion of grade inflation that went beyond the pale. A professor in a fairly esoteric branch of engineering, who was in a terminal contract year, taught a class of hundreds of students, many from outside of the college. When the final grades were turned in, just about everybody in the class received the highest grade possible. Sanctions were invoked, and this was the last instance that I am aware of in which the system simply broke down.

I can say, as a teacher myself, that the single hardest thing I do is to assign grades each semester. I have developed my own standards through the years that I use to guide my decision making. But the quality of the students we are getting at Notre Dame and I have had in my seminar has warranted giving fairly high grades rather consistently. Perhaps, without my knowing it, I, too, have a nickname that puts me in the company of Jake Kline, Father Brennan, and Father Murray. It wouldn't be bad company to keep.

Brother Cosmas Guttly, C.S.C.

Brother Cosmas Guttly lived to the ripe old age of ninety-nine. In my time in the Congregation of Holy Cross he lived longer than any other Holy Cross religious I have known. During the last thirty or so years of his life he was best known as a holy man of prayer, a kind of living saint, revered by all the members of the local Holy Cross community. In the era before concelebrated Masses were authorized and became popular, Brother Cosmas would spend much of his day serving at the individual Masses of Holy Cross religious and others who came to the Basilica of the Sacred Heart. In addition, he assisted in the sacristy of the church and helped out where he could.

One day when I was still a relatively young priest in the Notre Dame community, Brother Cosmas asked me to hear his confession. My first instinct was to look behind me as if he had addressed me by mistake. It was as though Mother Teresa of Calcutta had asked me for the Sacrament of Penance. The manifest holiness of the penitent stood in stark contrast in my own eyes to the unworthiness of the minister. In any case we successfully made our way through Brother Cosmas's recitation of sins. The whole experience was a reminder that the grace of the sacrament can flow both ways.

I once asked Brother Cosmas toward the end of his life what he thought the secret of longevity was. He recommended eating a banana a day and praying hard. Of course, we know from other evidence that good genes may be most important for a long life, together with the avoidance of stress and other factors. Since I am more partial to pears than bananas, I never followed his advice. However, I did accept his claim about the importance of prayer but have yet to approach his consistency and fervor. Despite Brother Cosmas's perspective on long life, it didn't enable him to make it to the grand age of one hundred. We were all rooting for him. The attendance at his funeral would suggest that we all thought we had picked up a bit of holiness by having him as a member of our local community.

Brother Cosmas was born in Switzerland, where he married and was widowed before immigrating to the United States and joining the Holy Cross community. While in the Swiss army, he had developed a reputation as a crack rifle shot. His primary work responsibility at Notre Dame was as a master toolmaker who put his skills to use in the College of Science. He also paid special attention to beautifying the area around the Grotto of Our Lady of Lourdes, one of the great places of campus pilgrimage.

Having been long impressed by Brother Cosmas's holiness and gentleness of spirit, I must admit to a certain degree of shock when I discovered that he would on occasion draw upon his proficiency as an ace rifleman. At times he would become frustrated by the damage that the squirrels and chipmunks were doing to the flowers and foliage near the Grotto. He would sneak out early in the morning with his rifle for a little target practice to reduce the number of attacking rodents. All of this was done as clandestinely and as quietly as possible (though one wonders how the shots were not heard). While Brother Cosmas did not share Saint Francis of Assisi's view of the animal kingdom, he was an effective protector of sacred space.

One more story about Brother Cosmas is worthy of telling. Once I was involved in a very distressing confrontation with a student who was becoming progressively more mentally ill. His rector and I and the counseling staff were obliged to tell him that his parents had agreed that he should withdraw from the university and begin a term of diagnosis and therapy at a mental health institution. In the midst of this encounter, the young man, in a fit of rage, slugged the rector and ran out of the counseling center. Since he had earlier made threats against some of his peers, we put out an all-points bulletin to University Security to be on the lookout for him. There was a great degree of anxiety that he might do harm to himself or to someone else.

After about an hour of searching, one of us remembered that the young man had had a number of worthwhile talks with Brother Cosmas. In the end he was found sitting quietly with Brother Cosmas in the crypt, the basement part of the church. He went calmly with the police and eventually was able to leave the campus and seek the help he so desperately needed. Brother's calming presence was critical in avoiding a physical encounter between Notre Dame Security and this sadly sick young man.

Brother Cosmas Guttly was a living saint who inspired us all. I am confident that he still prays for all of us as we continue our journeys.

Reverend John A. O'Brien

Father John A. O'Brien was a diocesan priest from Peoria who spent the last years of his ministry at Notre Dame. He was one of the first organizers of the Newman Club movement, which was intended to serve the spiritual, liturgical, and pastoral needs of Catholic students at secular colleges and universities. He served in this capacity for many years at the University of Illinois in Champaign-Urbana. In addition, Father O'Brien wrote a large number of popular theological books intended to help Catholics defend their faith against opponents and to attract others to think about joining the Catholic community. His most famous work, *Faith of Our Fathers*, was published in 1938 and remained a best seller for several years.

Father O'Brien came to Notre Dame at the invitation of Father Hesburgh after he got into a bit of a contretemps with his local bishop. His title was Theologian in Residence, and he lived in the Main Building. He was a very ascetic person who spent almost no money on himself. He once took a Continental scholar at Notre Dame, a man used to the finest restaurants of Paris and New York, out to dinner at the South Shore Line cafeteria. But as a diocesan priest, he was able to accrue and keep money that he had earned along the way. He was a shrewd investor in the stock market and over the course of time accumulated a substantial amount of money.

One of my memories of Father O'Brien from my student days is that he was always playing matchmaker between Notre Dame men and Saint Mary's College women. If he saw two people on his many walks around the campus who looked as though they might benefit from his matchmaking talent, he would simply introduce them to each other. He could get away with this social aggressiveness because his own persona was very upbeat and non-threatening. I remember him as a nice old man who was well liked by everyone, although few of us had any idea of exactly what he did.

As Father O'Brien grew into old age, he wanted to make provisions for his own medical care as his physical abilities declined. Eventually he discussed with Father Hesburgh and others the possibility of donating the money that he had amassed through the years to the university in exchange for access first to the Health Center and later to Holy Cross House, the community's health-care facility on campus. This was agreed to, and Father O'Brien eventually moved into Holy Cross House, where he resided until he died. As far as I know, he was the only non–Holy Cross resident ever to live in this wonderful facility.

After Father O'Brien was buried and his estate had been probated, the decision was made by Father Hesburgh, Father Joyce, and the university administration to divide the millions of dollars that he had left behind equally between the Departments of Theology and Philosophy. These monies were put into endowed professorships and endowed library collections. In my judgment this was one of the most crucial moves ever made by Notre Dame to enhance substantially the academic capabilities and reputation of the university in its two most pivotal departments. From that time until today, Theology and Philosophy have generally been regarded as the two best departments in the university. We have been able to attract outstanding faculty from this country and abroad as well as top-rate graduate students.

Anyone who met Father O'Brien during his lifetime would never have imagined that he would leave such a fortune behind. And it is ironic that a man often criticized during his life for "unscholarly" writing ended up contributing so much to the intellectual program of Notre Dame. But his love for Notre Dame, which supported him at a period when he was going through a great degree of personal distress, has reaped great benefits for the university, its faculty, and its students. May he rest in peace.

Mac McAllister

In some areas of Notre Dame life, a few individuals have attained legendary status. One of these was Mac McAllister, a short and skinny man with a sometimes colorful vocabulary, who for many years served as the athletic equipment manager. I came to know him when I joined the university community as a scholarship basketball player. At the beginning of the practice season we had to present ourselves at an assigned time to the equipment area, where Mac presided with almost tyrannical zeal. He took no guff from anyone, and he particularly prided himself on his ability to deal with what he took to be the most egotistical of the student athletes. To say that he was intimidating to a freshman athlete would be understating the case.

At the beginning of the practice season he would give you a pair of basketball shoes and a one-day supply of green practice shirt and shorts, along with a pair of socks. At the end of the daily practice, the presumption was that, after showering, you would put your sweaty equipment in the locker, where it would remain overnight. The next day, before practice, you would return the items to the equipment room and be given clean replacements.

Since there was a certain status in being seen on campus in a green athletic T-shirt, most of the student athletes found a way of not turning in their shirts before practice but making it appear that they had done so. If you could beat the system a couple times, then you would have a supply of green T-shirts to wear around the campus. Because the dirty clothes remained overnight in the confined locker space, they tended to smell to high heavens. Once you had your illicit supply of green shirts, you would put your laundry number on them and hand them in each week at the regular laundry pickup time. They would then come back with the other laundered clothes. But Mac was on to us, so before the end of each semester he would contact the laundry and retrieve all of the green T-shirts on a particular date. The only athletes who had beaten the system were those who did not turn in their laundry that week. This sort of game went on year after year during my four years as an under-graduate athlete.

In addition to the regular green T-shirt battles, Mac was a hard person to convince that you needed new basketball shoes. Though they might be frayed at the edges or slightly torn at the seams, this was not considered evidence enough, unless you happened to be a starter. Mac did not believe in superfluities. Our game uniforms tended to be plain, especially in comparison to what prevails today. (When we traveled on the road, we didn't have any special outfits. We were expected to dress properly, which meant wearing a sports jacket and a tie.) The same spartan standards prevailed when it came to the provision of towels and soap in the locker rooms. Mac believed in relatively small and thin towels, since they were easier to launder. He didn't concern himself with whether they were efficient drying tools for sometimes extraordinarily tall human beings.

I once saw Mac lose his cool when one of our more problem-filled players gave him some lip. He picked up a paperweight and threw it with vehemence in the direction of the athlete. Mac possessed an accurate arm, so the paperweight merely put a hole in the wall a few feet from the player's head. Never again did any of us show Mac McAllister anything other than the greatest respect.

Brother Movie:
Robert O'Brien, C.S.C.

In my days as a student, one of the highlights on Saturday nights was the showing of first-run commercial films in Washington Hall. Since they were free, going to the movies was a very popular activity; and for those involved with women from Saint Mary's College, it was a cheap date. Gathering so many students in a confined space meant that they tended to be exuberant and full of energy. Even with the best of movies this could mean wisecracks, hisses, and catcalls from the audience. In order to control these outbursts, Brother Robert O'Brien, C.S.C., was assigned to keep order. Brother Robert was quite elderly and walked with the assistance of a cane. If he thought that things had gotten out of hand, he would motion to the projectionist to stop the film, mount the stage to castigate those involved, and even threaten to cancel the movie. Because he exercised this critical role week after week, Brother Robert got to be known affectionately as Brother Movie. No one quite knew where he lived or anything about his personal background; for us he had only one purpose in life. He was a sword hanging over our Saturday night fun. However, Brother Movie was smart enough not to overstep his bounds. As far as I know, he never canceled a film. But his brinksmanship was a reminder that persistent crowd misbehavior would cost us.

Brother Bookstore:
Conan Moran, C.S.C.

A longtime manager of the bookstore, Brother Conan Moran, C.S.C., began his work when the bookstore was only a couple of rooms on the first floor of Badin Hall. He led the transition to the modern Hammes Bookstore between Walsh and Badin Halls, which served the Notre Dame community so well for many decades. Because the expanded bookstore was a magnet for many visitors to the university, Brother Conan became one of the legendary campus agents of hospitality. He developed personal relationships with Notre Dame people over the years, especially on football weekends. His hard work and devotion to duty is still remembered by countless generations of students, graduates, and friends.

My relationship with Brother Conan involved a lot of kidding. He saw his major responsibility as maximizing the bookstore's contribution to the university's budget, and I would rib him about rumors of impending sales at reduced prices. His response was always, "over my dead body." With the passage of the years, Brother Conan was forced to hand over the supervision of the bookstore to others, but he retained a special interest in the operation. When he finally died, I had the privilege of celebrating the Mass and preaching at his funeral. In addition to celebrating his life as a Holy Cross brother and a wonderful human being, I also seized the opportunity to recall our frequent conversations. I said with reverent humor that as Brother Conan's body was carried off to be buried in the community cemetery, I, in my capacity as president of the university, was going to declare a sale in the bookstore.

Portraits from the Corby Hall Gallery

Corby Hall, which is connected by a walkway to Sacred Heart Basilica and which once served as an undergraduate dormitory, is the headquarters of the Holy Cross community at Notre Dame. It is the residence of the religious superior and also provides housing for about twenty members of the community who are either semi-retired or no longer live in the student dormitories.

Comfortable, but not fancy, it is a place for community gatherings and a center of hospitality for members of the congregation or guests from outside Notre Dame. It includes a chapel, in which the community gathers for prayer several times each day; a dining room for breakfast and dinner; a snack bar where lunch is available; and a small laundry with two washers and two dryers. It also holds a number of offices where the various details of community life can be attended to.

Members of the university tend to think of Corby Hall as a kind of physical symbol of the Holy Cross community's presence on campus, much as the Dome is thought of as representing the administration. The community itself has a wide variety of personality types, political and theological orientations, work responsibilities, and years of service at the institution. Despite the differences in perspective on just about anything, the general spirit at Corby Hall is positive and reinforcing. We collectively recognize the truth (even though sometimes we have to be reminded of it) that we are stronger together and more effective in ministry than we would ever be singly. The Holy Cross community at Notre Dame, as the founding religious order, has a special affinity for the place.

Outside of the entrance to the chapel in Corby Hall on both walls are several framed picture albums with a series of 2 x 4 cards of remembrance in chronological order. Each of the cards has a small picture of one of the 302 Holy Cross priests and brothers of the Indiana Province who have died since 1960 together with their birth and death dates, the time of final procession, and, for the priests, the date of ordination. No other biographical details are included. Beside the photo case closest to the chapel entrance is a small month's mind box, where the names of those who have died on the current date are put. The tradition is to read these names and to remember them in prayer as one goes into the chapel. In this way, in addition to remembering in Vespers the members of the congregation who have died on that day, we pray for our members now deceased.

It seems appropriate to have this intimate connection with our colleagues and friends from the province who have gone before us as we continue to be inspired by their example. These are my reflections on those pictured in the photo case who have served at the university since my arrival as a student in 1959.

The Long-Lived Ones: Father Con Hagerty, a longtime professor of philosophy and one of the more conservative members of the community, lived to the age of ninety. He was very unhappy with the reforms of Vatican II and offered during his later years at Holy Cross House a continual commentary about how things were going to hell in a basket. To have some control over his final funeral liturgy, he got the provincial to pledge that it would be celebrated in Latin and that a Gregorian-chant choir would sing his favorite hymns. When the day arrived for his funeral liturgy, everything was going as he had specified until the celebrant, who had not said a Latin Mass for quite awhile, skipped over one whole page in the liturgical book and omitted the consecration entirely. Only after our superior general reminded the presider of his mistake were we able to have a valid liturgy. Moreover, the choir of priests was a bit rusty and not always in tune. Father Hagerty would have been happy with the intention but not with the execution.

A second nonagenarian was Father Sal Fanelli, who lived to the ripe old age of ninety-one. He had earned his undergraduate degree from Notre Dame but spent most of his apostolic ministry in pastoral work, principally at Saint Joseph's Parish nearby in South Bend. Sal was a wonderful, holy, and much beloved priest who developed the habit after he was ordained of counting all of the Masses he celebrated and all of the Communions he distributed, not to speak of baptisms, weddings, and funerals. He was known to bring a clicker with him to the confessional box and keep a tally of all the confessions he heard. When we make an account of ourselves at the final judgment, Sal will be well prepared.

The third and final long-lived community member was Brother Cosmas Guttly, who lived to the age of ninety-nine. As far as I know, he was the longest surviving member of the Indiana Province in its history. He had been married and served in the German army, and after his wife died he emigrated to the United States and joined the community as a Holy Cross brother. He was a technician in the science labs and after he retired was well known as sacristan in the parish and in Sacred Heart Basilica. (A longer account of his years of service is provided above.)

Former Provincials: Father Howard Kenna had a variety of administrative responsibilities during his time of public ministry. He was the vice president of Graduate Studies at Notre Dame for many years, served as the president of the University of Portland, and was elected provincial during probably the most tumultuous time in the modern history of religious life. He was provincial after Vatican II when a number of people left religious life and the priesthood and when many of the traditional rules and regulations as well as the power of religious leaders were being called into question. He was a man of deep faith and of real love of the community. He could appear stern, but in his dealings with individual community members, especially those who were most troubled during that difficult time, he was compassionate, supportive, and a real agent of God's love. During my days as a seminarian I was called to meet with Father Kenna, who was the same height both sitting and standing. (He had a large torso and small legs.) He told me during one visit that if I wanted to reform the community and the Church, I should do it from within and by established processes. It was good advice. When he died there was a tremendous outpouring of affection for him and the role that he had played in a challenging era. Among those present for the wake and funeral were many who had left the community during his period of leadership. They wanted to express how much he had meant to them during their journey of discernment.

Another provincial who has died since the 1960s was Father Bill Lewers, who came to the community late in life after joining the Law School faculty at the University of Illinois. After ordination, he taught at the Law School and later was the director of the Justice and Peace Office at the U.S. Bishops' Conference in Washington, D.C. During his time as provincial he was a great advocate for our institutional commitments as well as for our outreach and social justice ministry to the poor and dispossessed. He was a man of progressive ideas, with a full appreciation of the historical commitments of the province, and a thoughtful interpreter of current events in society and the Church.

Youthful Deaths: In the early history of the congregation at Notre Dame, mosquito-borne diseases and problems related to health and safety sometimes led to the premature loss of community members. With the passage of time, such events have become less commonplace. But recalled in the photos are several deaths that now seem premature and tragic. Father Denny Freemal, who was educated at Notre Dame and taught at Notre Dame High School, died in a traffic accident in Chicago at the age of thirty-one. Mike Rosing was on a summer service project in Mexico as a seminarian when he drowned in a river at the age of twenty-one. Father Mike McCafferty, a recognized candidate for the presidency of Notre Dame, died of cancer at forty-one; he was teaching at the Law School and was a very popular pastoral figure and mentor. Father Tom Oddo, then the president of the University of Portland and also a popular leader and community figure, died at the age of forty-eight in a tragic accident not far from the Portland campus. Tom and I were ordination classmates and close friends, and I had the privilege of preaching at his memorial Mass on our campus.

Bishops: Bishop Ed Heston, bright and well educated with degrees in civil and canon law, served the community for many years from his vantage point at the Generalate in Rome. John Cardinal O'Hara, former president of Notre Dame, former head of the Military Ordinariate, former bishop of Buffalo, and cardinal archbishop of Philadelphia, is buried in one of the alcoves of Sacred Heart Basilica. My room in Sorin Hall was his former room and the center of his pastoral ministry for several generations of students. Bishop Larry Graner served with distinction in Bangladesh and was a public and courageous critic of the government injustices that were perpetrated there. Archbishop Mark McGrath, who held both American and Panamanian citizenship because of his family background, was one of the theological and ecclesial leaders in the post–Vatican II reforms in Latin America as archbishop of Panama. He also served for many years on the Board of Trustees at Notre Dame, and he was responsible for the large number of Panamanians who have attended the university through the years. Bishop Vince McCauley was a missionary in Uganda and helped to mediate the transition in the post–Vatican II era from a primarily expatriate episcopal group to one that is now entirely made up of native Ugandan bishops. Vince is held in high regard as a saintly figure by the present generation of Ugandan Catholics. Bishop Paul Waldschmidt was the longtime president of the University of Portland and served as auxiliary bishop of the Diocese of Portland for many years.

Disciplinarians: There is no more difficult and important role that Holy Cross priests have been asked to play at Notre Dame than to be what was once called dean of students. Two who did so with distinction were Father Charlie McCarragher, who died at the age of seventy-eight, and Father Leonard Collins, who died at sixty-six. Charlie was known to make the circuit of the South Bend area on weekends and could easily strike fear in the heart of any offending undergraduate. He once told me how much he loved our students, but since the community and university had called him as dean, he knew that they would always regard him more as a figure of authority than as someone who was concerned for their welfare. Leonard Collins bore a similar burden, at least in the view of the student body. I once was summoned to his office, and he hardly looked up from his desk as he discussed some unacceptable behavior that I had been involved in. He, too, was a man who did his job because of a sense of duty rather than because he relished having to punish those students who did not meet the high standards of the University of Notre Dame.

Academicians: Many Holy Cross priests and brothers have served with distinction as part of the faculty at Notre Dame. In this section, I would like to recall four of them.

Father Tony Lauck died at the age of ninety-three. He was a priest-artist who produced during his lifetime a number of memorable pieces of sculpture as well as the stained-glass windows in the Moreau Seminary Chapel. Tony was a kind and gentle man who was instrumental in developing the collection that provided the foundation for the Snite Museum of Art. His Madonna statue lies at the northern side of the circle at the main entrance to the campus in a straight line with the statue of Father Sorin, the statue of the Sacred Heart, and the statue of the Blessed Virgin on top of the Dome. He was a man of simple tastes and lived most of his life with the seminarians at Moreau Seminary, yet he was quite popular among a certain crowd of art collectors in New York City and elsewhere. He also served for many years as the chaplain of the Ladies of Notre Dame and Saint Mary's College.

Father Mark Fitzgerald died at the age of ninety-five. An economist, he directed the Center on Labor-Management Relations at Notre Dame for many years. During the summer he would welcome representatives of some of the major American unions and try to bring them together with labor negotiators and management representatives. Mark was a dedicated runner and outdoorsman. Even into his late seventies and early eighties he could be seen jogging around the old Notre Dame golf course.

Father Ray Cour, a political science professor, died at eighty-six. He was one of the best-organized people I have ever met, and every aspect of his daily and weekly life was planned to the minute. For a number of years he served as the rector of Moreau Seminary and managed to balance his responsibilities there with his teaching obligations. In semi-retirement he was a generous chaplain in the downtown chapel in South Bend and also served the needs of the infirmary of the Holy Cross brothers at Holy Cross College.

Father John Burke died at the age of eighty-seven. A mathematician, he had the amazing ability to teach even those graduate students who were math-phobic. He saw it as his special duty to enable every Notre Dame undergraduate to pass the math requirement, and he spent hour after hour in his room in Corby Hall tutoring students. He represented the best tradition of professors' commitment to the needs and well-being of the students entrusted to their care.

Rectors: Countless Holy Cross priests and brothers have served as rectors on campus as part of the residential tradition of the university. Each of them would be worthy of attention in their own right. I'll simply focus on three as a representative sampling.

Father Jim Buckley died at the age of seventy-two after a bout of cancer. He was a philosopher by training, but sometime in mid-career he became known as a very able pastoral counselor. Despite something of a stuttering problem, he still managed to communicate effectively.

Father Larry Broestl died at the age of seventy. His nickname was "Brush" because he always wore his hair in a brush cut. He was the rector of Dillon Hall for many years and was famous for having memorized the names of all of his students by the end of the first week of school—quite an achievement, since at that time, Dillon was the largest dorm on campus. A smoker, Larry liked to start the day by hanging out at The Huddle, where he would drink coffee, smoke, and interact with the students. He was also a professor of German and combined in a happy way the multiple commitments that are typical of the Holy Cross religious on campus.

Father Joe Haley died at seventy-two. He was the rector in Farley Hall when I was a first-year student. He was affectionately known as "mumbles" because he never clearly enunciated his words. I remember him as a kind and committed individual who enforced the rules but never too rigorously. As it did for many rectors, the story circulated that sometimes he wore a leather shoe and a sneaker so that he could come down the corridor twice as fast after lights were out to catch students breaking the rules in one way or another.

Campus Ministry: Once again, many Holy Cross priests and brothers have been active in Campus Ministry. In the present day, its staff has grown substantially, as has the service that they render. Two Holy Cross priests will represent two different eras.

Father Bill Toohey died of meningitis at the age of fifty. He was the head of Campus Ministry in the era after Vatican II when liturgical reforms were being implemented, theological controversy was commonplace, and many styles of ministerial engagement were being experimented with. A handsome former Marine, Bill was a highly visible campus figure and an eloquent preacher. He had a special concern for social justice issues and tried to prepare the students and others for a new notion of the Catholic Church in the American context. He helped many students keep a place in the Church in the face of endless controversy.

Father Charlie Carey died at the age of ninety. I knew him primarily during the years when he lived in Corby Hall and was regularly visited by a host of former student friends. Of a traditional bent, he was a great and warm human being and someone whom others sought out in times of difficulty and tragedy. Many people came to him to take instruction, and he was often seen on the porch of Corby Hall working his way through the Catechism with them. Charlie was far from a fuddy-duddy, and he enjoyed the opportunity to have a drink or dinner somewhere in town with friends. When he died, he was held in the highest regard by his fellow Holy Cross religious.

Administrators: From the earliest days of Notre Dame, Holy Cross priests and brothers have served in administrative roles from president to various levels of vice president to other managerial tasks and assignments.

Father John Van Wolvlear died at the age of seventy-three. He was a very athletic and gregarious person who served for a number of years as vice president for Student Affairs. Earlier in his life he was in a major accident in the Alps and spent a long time in recovery. John never took himself too seriously and always sought to serve the best interest of the students. He was great company, and he died as he would have liked, playing tennis with some friends and ahead on the score.

Father Jerry Wilson died at the age of seventy-seven and was for many years vice president for Business Affairs. He oversaw many of the concrete needs of the campus community, but especially the business operations and the physical plant. Jerry never complained but just did his job as efficiently and helpfully as possible. On the day that he officially retired as vice president, I talked him into letting me take a group of seminarians on a tour up into the Dome and inside the statue of the Blessed Virgin. I am sure that Jerry died a thousand deaths worried that we would either be discovered or suffer some accident. (See "Inside the Dome.")

Father Paul Beichner was a professor of English and a medieval scholar. He served for many years as vice president of Graduate Studies. He was also an accomplished artist who delighted in trying to capture a bit of the animal kingdom and did sketches of some of his fellow Holy Cross community members. Paul truly appreciated the life of the mind and did everything he could to foster Notre Dame's development as a research university.

Father Chet Soleta died at the age of eighty-six. He was a very popular English professor for many years and then became vice president of Graduate Studies. Later in life, he became pastor of Sacred Heart Parish and was known as an excellent preacher and a man completely sympathetic with the reforms of Vatican II. His hobby was gardening, and he could often be seen outdoors tending to the flowers in the spring and summer.

Father Ferd Brown died at the age of eighty-four. For many years he was vice president and associate provost, assisting in the Provost's Office, particularly on the financial side. He was a mathematician by training and brought acumen with numbers and accounts books to ensure that the academic side of the university would live within its budget. For one period, he also was acting provost and was committed to achieving a smooth transition in that office. Later, Ferd served as local superior of the Holy Cross community.

Missionaries: From the earliest days of Father Sorin, Notre Dame sent some of its best members off on missions, either in this country or to other parts of the world. As a result, there has always been a strong orientation toward the world Church by the local religious community. Our familiarity with various countries like India, Bangladesh, Kenya, Uganda, Chile, Peru, Haiti, Brazil, and Ghana was higher than that of the average American because we knew people who were living and working there. One missionary who had a profound impact on our local community was Father Ed Goedert, who died at the age of seventy-eight. Ed was a traditional missionary, in the best sense of the term, in

Bangladesh for much of his adult life. He once said that he had suffered from dysentery every day that he had served there. Nevertheless, while he was working in a parish in the outlying areas during the civil war when Bangladesh split off from West Pakistan, he often had to provide basic support for tens of thousands of refugees fleeing the violence. He did the best he could with help from the rest of the Holy Cross religious there. Finally, his health demanded that he return to the States, and he came to Notre Dame as an associate pastor in Sacred Heart Parish. He was thin, almost emaciated looking, but a great storyteller and a very effective fundraiser for the missions. While he was chary of telling too many war stories, he often regaled us, when pushed, with descriptions of his experiences.

Special Cases: In this category I will include individuals who by bent of personality, talent and distinctive style made a huge mark on the university and the broader community.

Father Charley Sheedy died at the age of seventy-eight. He was a professor of moral theology in the Theology Department and later served for many years as dean of the College of Arts and Letters. An avid reader and a talented golfer, he was also very idiosyncratic in his manner and in his propensities. He was one of the most astute judges of character that I ever met. Charley was a recovering alcoholic and spent many years helping others to deal with the same affliction. In his later years, he continued to teach and was part of the staff at Moreau Seminary. For many in my generation, he was probably our favorite Holy Cross priest and represented the best combination of a deep rooting in the past and an openness of mind and spirit about the future. He never put on airs. Once, toward the end of his teaching career, the day before his first class of the semester he said to me that he didn't have anything to say. I advised him to go in, after teaching for forty or fifty years, and just do the best he could. Of course, the students were enthralled.

Father Louie Putz died at the age of eighty-nine. He had emigrated to the United States from Germany as a boy. Louie was a believer in movement and was a great initiator. He started Fides Press, which was dedicated to publishing high-quality theological books, especially those translated from European languages. He founded YCS (Young Christian Students) on campus, which led many of its participants into other forms of service after graduation. After writing a book about reforming seminaries, he was made rector of Moreau Seminary and served in that capacity while I was studying theology on campus. Later in life, he began a program of continuing education for senior citizens in the

South Bend area and encouraged many Notre Dame faculty to teach there. To this day that program continues in the former school of St. Patrick's Parish on Western Avenue. I also remember that Louie was the world's worst driver, although he claimed that he had never had an accident. Most of us imagined all the other cars on the road smashing into each other to avoid his heavy foot.

Father John Gerber died at the age of sixty-five after a struggle with cancer. John taught English, although he never finished his doctorate. He was a man of deep prayer who conquered a number of demons in his life and who was a prized and trusted spiritual director. He served as local superior at Corby Hall and also as assistant provincial. For a period of time, he ministered to the Native Americans in one of the tribes in Arizona. He tried a number of experiments in his life in terms of forms of ministry and living situations. In the end he was remembered as a good and holy religious who fashioned his own style of ministry here on campus and in the broader American Catholic Church.

OF THIS AND THAT

The Lucky Trumpeter

A member of the Notre Dame marching band had taken his trumpet home to play Taps at his grandfather's funeral. It seems that his grandfather had served in the army, and members of the family thought that Taps would be a fitting tribute. On his way back from the funeral, the student was pulled over, somewhere in southern Michigan, by a state trooper for going eighty-two miles per hour in a seventy-mile-per-hour zone. When the officer saw the trumpet in the back seat, he asked the student if he was a member of the Notre Dame Marching Band. The student explained that he had been speeding back to the university because he was going to be late for the home football game.

The state trooper took the student's license and registration and went back to his patrol car. Meanwhile, the young man sat in his car fretting over the forthcoming court date and fine. When the trooper returned, he said, "If you do me a favor, I won't write you a ticket. Do you know how to play the Notre Dame Fight Song?" The student quickly answered, "Yes, of course." "Will you play it on my radio to my co-workers who are huge Irish fans, just like me? Sound like a deal?" The student quickly assented and played the best Fight Song rendition he could muster to the listening group of police officers, who proceeded to cheer after he had finished. The officer then shook the student's hand and told him he was sorry about his grandfather and to drive safely back to Notre Dame. Such was the good fortune of one lucky trumpeter.

The Scary Confessor

When I was an undergraduate at Notre Dame, most students worshiped on the weekend in Sacred Heart Basilica. As was the custom of the day, priests were available in both transepts and in the rear of the church to hear confessions, both before and during Mass. As was true in larger parishes, certain confessors developed reputations for being either easier or harder in their interaction with the penitent. Some were known for asking a lot of questions, and others for assigning more rigorous penances. For many of us, the ideal confessor was slightly hard of hearing, forgiving of human frailty, and inclined to assign a relatively modest penance.

One Sunday morning I was in a rather long line on the right-hand side waiting to go to confession to Father Joe Barry. A chaplain in the Second World War, he was known to be very down-to-earth and approachable. Everyone assumed that nothing could shock him and that he was innately tolerant of human weakness. The confessor on the left-hand side, who will remain nameless, had the opposite reputation. He was known to be inquisitive, rigorous, and intent on shaking the penitent out of his or her complacency.

On this given Sunday, there were relatively long lines of ten or fifteen people behind each of the confessionals. Father Barry's line was moving along smoothly, but it seemed as if the first person who had gone into the other booth was there for a long time. Then, all of a sudden, we heard in muffled tones, "You did what?" The students turned their attention to the booth of the anonymous priest. All of a sudden, there was a slamming of the sliding door in front of the grille through which the penitent spoke to the confessor. Then a red-faced student emerged. Meanwhile, everyone who had been waiting in that line quickly transferred themselves over to Father Barry's confessional. As I remember, no one took the place of those who had been standing on the left-hand side.

None of us had any idea of what might have transpired between the penitent and the unnamed priest, but it was clear to all of us that the better part of valor was to move to the other line. Whether the priest had had a bad day or the penitent had confessed some horrible crime did not matter. We knew that everyone could be forgiven their sins by Father Barry without either losing face or being subjected to a tongue-lashing. One thinks, of course, of the interaction of Jesus in the Gospels with sinners where he shows sensitivity and compassion. Fortunately, in all my penitential experiences at Notre Dame, I never had to face a scary confessor. And on that day, neither did anyone else.

The Headless Statue

One winter in the mid-1990s a severe ice storm hit the campus. The ice came in the wake of several storms that had left a white cover of snow on the campus grounds. Many power lines were downed, and driving was extremely perilous on the roads into and out of the campus. The combination of wind and cold brought down a great number of trees and branches.

This sort of winter outbreak is not unprecedented, as any Notre Dame person can recall. We have survived in our history numerous windstorms, snowstorms, ice storms, and blizzards. But what was note-worthy about this particular storm was that the statue of the Sacred Heart, which lies immediately south of the Main Building, had toppled over and—it appeared—had lost its head as it lay buried in the snow. This particular statue with its patina has always been a favorite of the thousands of students who pass by it each week. Its Latin inscription, *Venite Ad Me Omnes* (Come everyone to me), is a reference to the biblical passage in Matthew where Jesus urges all those who carry heavy bur-dens to come to Him because His yoke is easy and His burden is light. Now a kind of panic set in, as if this were a bad omen. The leadership of the Senior Class volunteered to provide funds to help put the head back on the statue and re-erect it. Other members of the Notre Dame com-munity had heard the news and were interpreting it in similarly dire terms. Some worried that a wire-service photo would symbolize to Notre Dame critics the fate of Catholicism on campus.

None of these observers had noted that as the statue fell, it simply went head first into the snow, which was six or seven inches deep. In fact, the head was still attached but wasn't visible to those who walked by in a hurry. When the grounds crew assessed the damage, they could see that all that was needed was some kind of hoisting device to pick up the statue and place it back in its original position. This restoration was achieved rather quickly, and soon the word spread around the campus that the Sacred Heart was back to normal. I never did find out whether the Senior Class leadership thought that we had performed some miracle, in record time, to reattach the head. In any case, this incident was a fitting reminder that Notre Dame's people don't like ominous messages from the heavens.

The Blizzard of '78

One of the most persistent memories for Notre Dame graduates has to do with the constant battle against the frigid winter weather. Students from warm climates learn early the importance of wearing layered clothing and keeping the head and the extremities as warm as possible. During the winter, in the midst of endless dreary, cold, and windswept days and nights, it is important to remember that spring, with all of its beauty, will eventually arrive.

When Father Sorin and his Holy Cross brother companions arrived on the South Bend frontier for the first time in November 1842, the site of today's campus was covered with snow, and it was impossible for the new arrivals to discern that there were two separate lakes. This led to the French misdescription, which officially titles the university "Notre Dame du Lac" (of the lake, that is, of one lake). The winter of 1842 was subsequently considered one of the coldest and snowiest on record. This led to the perennial joke that the Holy Cross community planned to move on once the snow melted, but it never did.

Each generation of Notre Dame students has its own tales of wintry woe to tell. In some years the absence of sun for weeks at a time is noteworthy. In other years it might be an occasional ice storm or persistent rains in the springtime. Some remember sitting outdoors at home football games in the worst playing conditions. But generally, the most often-recounted stories have to do with blizzards.

It was the academic year 1977–78 that set the modern-day record for the most snow in one winter season. The final tally of total inches was 172! There was even a contest in downtown South Bend in a big empty lot, where a lot of the snow from the streets had been dumped, about when the last remnants would melt. (It turned out to be sometime in July.) In that record-setting winter, it was four days in January that stood out. Winds reached 52 miles an hour, the temperature dipped to 8 degrees, with a wind-chill of minus 26 degrees and a low barometer of 28.84. Forty-one inches of snow fell between January 26 and January 29, paralyzing northwest Indiana. For the first time in its history, Notre Dame was closed for five straight days, including a weekend. South Bend was impassable, and all travel was prohibited in St. Joseph County except for snowmobiles. Notre Dame employees in the dining halls and in other essential operations were unable to go back and forth to their homes, and it became necessary to put them up in temporary shelters on campus.

It was impossible to hold classes during the days in which travel was precluded, so school was called off. Large front-end loaders began the process of cleaning off the roads on campus and the parking lots, but much of this activity was limited because of the number of vehicles stuck in the lots and around the campus. By the third or fourth day of the storm, some of the arterial roads opened, at least in one lane. This allowed some of our students to make it off campus to try to resupply their caches of food and drink. As more and more people suffered from cabin fever, there were snowball fights and other high jinks.

A men's basketball game between Notre Dame and the University of Maryland already had been scheduled. The Michiana Regional Airport reopened, and the Maryland team foolishly agreed to abide by their commitment. Father Hesburgh flew in on a plane with the television announcers for the game. The broader Notre Dame community was notified that anyone who could make it to the Joyce Center would be admitted for free. By the time the game began, the basketball arena at the Joyce Center was packed with rabid and stir-crazy fans. The noise level set new records for decibels of enthusiasm. Suffice it to say that the Maryland team did not have a chance. The Notre Dame basketball team emerged victorious, 69–54.

There have been other years when the snowfall was almost as large and significant in total inches, but never again has Notre Dame experienced such a concentrated period of relentless and heavy snow and blowing wind. While the Blizzard of 1978 did disrupt campus life for a period, it stands as a great bragging point for those who can legitimately say that their days at Notre Dame were the most challenging and bleakest ever.

The Peripatetic Car

The following story is true. The names have been changed to protect the innocent.

Father X might best be described as a hard-working, orderly person who is not easily flustered and certainly not inclined to high jinks. He makes friends easily, and sometimes these friends may try to take advantage of his gentleness of spirit. Now, Father Y and Father Z are peers of Father X. They are both well respected and active in the Notre Dame community. Father Y, in particular, has an elfin quality about him and likes to periodically break up the routines of life with some unsuspected humor. The critical element in Father Y's talent as a troublemaker is that the victim seldom expects what's going on or knows who is involved. Father Z has a comparable spirit of lightheartedness, especially in dealing with community members of a more somber visage, but he usually has to be drawn into mischief by Father Y.

Father X was accustomed to parking his car in one of the reserved spaces in front of Corby Hall. When Father X went away on a trip, Father Z asked if he could borrow his car. Father X agreed, and Father Y had the car keys duplicated. After Father X returned, every couple of days, Father Y or Father Z would move the car a few places away from where Father X had parked it. At first, he either did not notice or thought that one of the young men who fill up the cars with gas had parked it in a different spot. This occurred three or four times, and Father X was beginning to suspect that something was wrong. Then, several days later, the car was parked not in front of Corby Hall but behind it, leading its owner to search high and low before finding it. Once again, he was suspicious but did not draw the connection to his friends.

This conspiracy came to a head one day when Father Z parked Father X's car perpendicular to the entrance to Sacred Heart Basilica. When the security patrols came along, they couldn't figure out what had happened since this is a high-traffic area in which no one in his right mind would park a car. When they reported the problem to Father X, he was beside himself. At this point, he began to put two and two together and decided that he had been had. When he confronted Fathers Y and Z, they admitted that they had been in cahoots. After a few words of reproof, Father X acknowledged their creativity as well as the fact that they had caught him off guard, thus proving that within a religious community there is the same kind of tomfoolery encountered elsewhere.

The Wrong Christmas Party

Several years ago, on the scheduled date for the Facilities Operations Christmas party, a major snowfall hit the campus. The party had to be cancelled because many of the people involved in snow removal were to have taken part in the celebration. I try to go to as many of these events as I can to thank our employees and faculty for the outstanding job that they do throughout the year. For some areas of the campus, the Christmas party is the best opportunity to thank these work units as a whole.

The year following the cancellation, I made a special effort to attend the Facilities Operations Christmas celebration. On the assigned day, I left my office early so that I could spend the full social hour with the participants. I went over to the concourse in the Joyce Center to chat with early arrivals. Then, in the course of the evening, I began to go from table to table wishing everyone a Merry Christmas and a Happy New Year. Everyone seemed delighted to see me, and I was pleased that the evening was going well.

When I had made my way to the final table, Dave Woods, who was a supervisor in the unit, came up to me and said, "I'm glad you finally arrived, the party is here in the Monogram Room." In some befuddlement, I asked who was having the party in the concourse. Dave replied that it was one of the small hospitals in the area. I then understood why several people had indicated that their spouses would be arriving late because they were still at the hospital. I had thought that perhaps there had been a bout of sickness in the group. One result of the evening, in which I greeted the local hospital as well as Facilities Operations, is that other entities outside of the university that host Christmas celebrations on our campus might now expect me to show up as a general gesture of good will and hospitality.

The Pastoral Key

During every Christmas season, Notre Dame's security police host a Mass for themselves in Sacred Heart Parish Center, followed by a reception and dinner. It takes place usually on the Saturday or Sunday before Christmas, after most of the Notre Dame community has gone home for the holidays. One year when I arrived to say Mass, I found that security chief Rex Rakow and his assistants had set up just about everything we needed for the liturgy. However, they could not find the key to the part of the sacristy where the chalice and paten are stored.

It is not unusual if you are helping out at a parish when the pastor is away to have to hunt for the key that opens the storage closet for the liturgical vestments as well as the tabernacle. You simply use your refined instincts as a Church person. After all, there are only so many hiding places in the sacristy. On this particular occasion, I tried to figure out where the key might be hidden. But after five or ten minutes of fruitless searching, I had a meeting of the minds, which included several individuals who had spent years in various police departments investigating crimes before they joined the Notre Dame department. It was like having six or seven Sherlock Holmeses all working on the same case. Nevertheless, after hunting in every logical place, we were still bamboozled. Finally, one of us checked a desk against the wall at the entrance of the church and across from the sacristy door. The key was finally located in one of the drawers. All this suggests is that sometimes it is easier to find the clues to solve a major crime than it is to find a key hidden by a shrewd pastor.

Busing the Wrestling Team

When the vice president of Student Affairs at Notre Dame, Father Mark Poorman, C.S.C., was serving as the rector of Dillon Hall, he was asked by the coach of the men's wrestling team to accompany its members on an extended trip to Florida. For family reasons, the coach had to be absent for part of the trip and that left Father Poorman in charge. One night, on the way back from a meet, the bus was driving through an urban neighborhood. The driver passed a woman in obvious distress who was trying to flag down the bus. Although initially the bus continued on, the students quickly decided to turn around and see if they could assist her. Once they opened the door, she readily jumped aboard. When they had a closer look and heard in relatively foul language her description of a fight in a bar from which she had just emerged, it became clear that she was a person experienced in drink and in being plucked from the streets.

As the bus moved on and she became aware that it was full of a group of attractive young men, she began to try to ingratiate herself as she made her way down the aisle. Father Poorman, who was not wearing his clerical collar, proceeded to introduce himself and the team: "I'm Father Mark Poorman and these are the members of the Notre Dame wrestling team." The woman looked up, considered what he had said, and then exclaimed, "This is living proof that I died in the bar fight and I've gone to Heaven."

Reading to Children

Several years ago, I decided that I would like to have the opportunity to come to the Early Childhood Development Center (ECDC) on campus at least once or twice per year to be together with the children there. Part of my motivation was the memory of our founder, Father Edward Sorin, C.S.C., who, late in his life, with his long white beard, was often pictured affectionately gathered with the minims (or grade-school children) of Notre Dame.

I'd had an earlier experience a number of years ago in going to a local elementary school where I read a story to the first-grade class. In that school setting I asked the children to play out the different roles in the story. One of the central characters was a cruel old man who was alienated from the rest of the village and went out of his way to be unkind to the children. A young boy agreed to take the part, so we asked him to go off to the far side of the classroom to act out the story. He was there only a few seconds when he started to cry because everybody hated him. The teacher suggested that we invite him back into the center of the group. I thus learned that you can only go so far in trying to achieve verisimilitude.

In order to prepare for my first reading venture at ECDC, I sought the advice of several members of our staff with young children and then asked the head of the school to send me five or six books so that I could make a selection. I chose two books for the two- and three-year-olds, and two books for the four- and five-year-olds. In my maiden ECDC experience, each of my reading groups sat in front of me with the teachers sitting protectively and confidently behind them. Both sets of children seemed to have heard the stories before, so they quickly got into the spirit of the moment. I had them making animal sounds and moving around a bit, but nothing too disruptive. My secretary had put together bags of little gifts so that each child could have a souvenir. Generally, I thought things went smoothly, and I returned to the campus pleased with the day.

The second year I was invited back, and I returned with a pretty high sense of confidence. Once again, I was sitting with the twos and threes reading two different stories, and things were going well. When I finished reading to the fours and fives, I handed each of the children their gift of the day. One of the kids looked into the bag and complained that they were getting the same kind they had been given last year. When I returned to the campus, I had to form a committee to decide how to handle this new crisis. Little did I know that I had to offer more variety if I were to gain acceptance year after year.

In the same vein, a couple of years ago I was invited by the director of the new Hammes Notre Dame Bookstore to come and read a children's version of the Nativity story a few days before Christmas. Since this was the first time this was undertaken, no one was sure how many children would show up. Despite the fact that the weather was cold and somewhat snowy, we had a good turnout. I was seated in a big chair next to a beautiful crèche scene. I decided for dramatic effect to take the image of the baby Jesus out of the crib and put it in my pocket so that at the appropriate time I could hold it in my hand and put it in the crib.

During the course of the story the children seemed attentive. As I approached the climax, I proceeded to hold the figure in my hand,

at which point a little boy cried out, "You've been sitting on the baby Jesus!" All of a sudden I knew that I had done something unacceptable in terms of the religious sensibilities of the group. I finessed my way out by saying that I had never really sat on it, but it was just in my pocket. In the end, I had them all come up and touch the image of baby Jesus and say a prayer.

The second year I was invited back by the bookstore and we had a different version of the Christmas story for children. This time there was an even bigger crowd together with a woman who helped us sing some carols during the reading. A pretty little blonde girl standing next to me offered to turn the pages. I asked her what role she was playing in the story, and she said that for a couple of chapters she was Joseph. Then later, when Mary began to take a more prominent role, she decided that she was tired of being Joseph and now wanted to be Mary. I was reminded that in the imagination of children all things are possible.

The Prophet of Yahweh

One of my most frequent correspondents for many years was a Notre Dame graduate from the 1950s, a successful businessman who claimed to be the Prophet of Yahweh. He not only wrote me but he also had corresponded with Father Ted Hesburgh regularly as well as with the local religious superior. One of his concerns in the Hesburgh era was that any change in leadership would lead to some kind of apocalyptic outcome. As a result, he used to circulate a petition at the Alumni Reunion weekends under the heading, "Hesburgh or Disorder." He would try to get signatures from the attendees to join the cause, and when I was still serving as vice president, I was familiar with this activity.

On the day after I was elected the sixteenth president of Notre Dame I received a parchment scroll in the mail. Its message, inscribed by a fancy pen, was full of quotes from the Hebrew prophets, all of which purported to prove that I deserved to be elected president and that the entrusted Prophet of Yahweh was giving me his approbation. At the bottom the author had signed it with his real name together with his assumed religious name, implying that he was speaking as Yahweh's messenger. Underneath his signature was an indication that copies had been sent to "Theodore M. Hesburgh, C.S.C., lame duck," and "Edmund P. Joyce, C.S.C., lame duck" (Hesburgh's executive vice president), among others. Seldom in the history of religion has a prophet changed his message so dramatically, almost overnight.

After I took office as president, I still received regular correspondence from the Prophet of Yahweh. He would often clip out articles about matters of religion or about people from Notre Dame and write comments of approval or disapproval in the margins. At first I used to write back in a fairly perfunctory way, but then I decided that he was going to continue no matter what I said, so I ceased responding. Then, one beautiful fall evening, Ted Hesburgh and I were leaving Corby Hall when we spotted the Prophet of Yahweh coming in our direction. We glanced at each other and, on the spur of the moment, redirected our paths at a right angle to avoid coming face-to-face with him. I never doubted his sincerity, but somehow I never thought that the legitimacy of my presidency depended on his validation.

The Greatest Gift

The Sunday 10 a.m. Mass from the Basilica of the Sacred Heart is broadcast on the Hallmark cable channel. The visual images from the Basilica are quite impressive, as are the beautiful music provided by the chapel choir and the preaching of the celebrants. Father Peter Rocca, C.S.C., rector of the Basilica, receives letters or e-mails on a regular basis from those who watch the Mass on television. Many are homebound, unable to attend their local parishes; others are Christians of various denominations who are moved by the prayerfulness of the liturgy or the message of the homily; still others are those who have questions about their Catholic faith.

Recently, Father Rocca received a letter from a young woman who is an inmate in a detention center because of her involvement in drugs. She is also the mother of a child who is being raised by relatives. The woman has begun to see her incarceration as a gift from God, a time in which she can work on putting her past behind her and start a new life both for herself and her son. She wrote that the Sunday Mass from the Basilica was the only one available to her; it brightened her week and had led her to recommit herself to the Christian faith. When she finishes her sentence at the detention center, she plans on attending Sunday Mass on a regular basis at her parish church. At the end of her letter she asked to have a Sunday missal sent to her so that she can better pray and follow the service. When Father Rocca sent the missal, he assured her of his prayers for her and her son. She wrote back that that was the greatest gift she could ever receive.

Flying for Notre Dame

Father Edward Sorin, C.S.C., the first president of Notre Dame, was reputed to have made more than fifty trips across the Atlantic during his term of service, first as president and then later as superior general of our religious community. This would be an extraordinary feat, even today, but in the nineteenth century it entailed an even more perilous set of steps in order not only to make it to the East Coast of the United States but also to survive the rigors of the North Atlantic.

In a sense, Father Sorin's peregrinations became a model for some of the subsequent presidents of the university. Father John Zahm, C.S.C., made a number of trips to Latin America and had a special interest in that region of the world. But it was really my immediate predecessor, Father Theodore Hesburgh, C.S.C., who set the new standard for presidential travel. During his thirty-five years in office, Father Ted crossed the globe and took a special delight in the number of countries he had visited. On one occasion, he was traveling in Colombia with another Holy Cross priest when on a full plane a drunken soldier armed with a rifle declared that he was going to hijack the aircraft. As would be imagined, the passengers were terrified. Fortunately, as time passed, the soldier grew groggy and eventually fell asleep. When the plane landed, security forces came aboard, took his gun away, and put him under arrest. After a minimal delay, the plane continued on to its destination. On another occasion, Father Hesburgh was flying in Alaska on a private plane when some disagreement arose between the chief pilot and the owner about whether the path to the landing place required skimming past an ice-covered mountain. Father Ted eventually convinced the pilot that his instincts were right and, as a result, they were able to avoid crashing head-on into the mountainside. The owner was not too happy with this manifestation of insubordination and subsequently fired the pilot. On a third occasion, Ted was flying in El Salvador as part of an international group overseeing the fairness of elections. At the time a civil war was raging between the military and a well-armed group of rebels.

In order to get to one of the outlying regions it was necessary to fly in a helicopter over disputed territory. As they took off, the helicopter pilot warned the passengers that they could be subject to gunfire from the ground. Each person looked around for something metallic to sit on as the next level of protection. Fortunately, the oversight mission returned to base without encountering any hostile fire.

In my own years as president, I, too, have traveled throughout the world. On my one trip to Africa, to the country of Cameroon, I discovered that the national airline was known to have a high accident rate and also to be unreliable in keeping to its schedule. In order to get from the port city of Douala to the capital city of Yaoundé, I waited around for almost twenty-four hours before I learned that the flight between the two cities might not take off for a couple of days. On my return trip, I decided to go by bus to Douala and once there to risk flying on a Cameroon Airlines 747 to Paris. I arrived in the airport in Douala hours ahead of time to find that there were hundreds of hangers-on all looking for action. As the hour for departure got closer, I grew more and more anxious. As I was finally going through security, I realized that the machine designed to ensure that no bombs or suspicious items were carried on board was not working. The agents had no backup plan, so they simply waved everyone through without checking any of the bags. The 747 finally was fully loaded, and when it took off I felt like kissing the floor of the plane, almost like Pope John Paul II, who for many years kissed the ground when he arrived in a new country. We reached Paris safely, and I decided never again to fly on a local African airline.

Notre Dame has made a variety of planes available for its officers, fund-raisers, and athletic coaches in my term as president. For many years we had a Cessna 310, a twin-engine plane with one pilot. Since the plane did not have the capacity to fly above the weather, we simply had to go through it. Our pilot at the time was Bill Corbett, a former Navy airman, who might best be described as dauntless and unperturbable. On occasion we would fly through the middle of thunderstorms with lightning flashing all around. Once we were flying into Kansas City's downtown airport when the control panel indicated that our landing gear was not properly locked. Bill flew over the air traffic controllers' tower and had them look up to see whether they thought there was an instrument malfunction. The controllers decided that the landing gear looked safe, and we were able to land without difficulty.

Later we had an upgrade to a plane with two pilots. Coming back from Washington, D.C., one time, we had a clear indication that the landing gear was not locked. An air traffic control tower in West Virginia confirmed our situation. We kept on flying toward South Bend. At one point, the co-pilot, Pat Farrell, had to go down into the innards of the plane and hand crank the landing gear down. Meanwhile, we were getting closer to our destination and were low on fuel. As we prepared to descend into South Bend, I could see the emergency trucks lined up along the runway. A couple of minutes out the panel indicated that the landing gear was finally locked, so it turned out that we were okay. The emergency vehicles accompanied us down the runway. I was very happy to greet the person in charge of the rescue crews by walking out the main door.

I have great admiration for the high quality of the pilots who have worked for the university through the years. I have entrusted my life and that of many other members of our community to their expertise and skill. Like police work, flying can be very routine in most situations, but it is when the circumstances or weather turn threatening or foul that all of the training and skills of the pilots come to the fore. God willing, we will continue to fly safely in order to tell the Notre Dame story around the world and to forge strong bonds with our graduates and friends.

A Night in New York City

Not all of the most interesting and exciting Notre Dame stories take place on campus. As a lover of big cities and a person with some professional credentials in the area of police ethics, I have always been somewhat of an ambulance chaser. Because of the size, diversity, and importance of New York City, I have always enjoyed my trips there, especially when they gave me the opportunity to walk the streets and experience some of the dynamism of the Big Apple.

One of our longtime trustees, now deceased, was Tom Coleman, an investment banker and bachelor who inherited from his father a role on the New York City Police and Fire Boards. As a result, he came to know many of the leaders of those departments as well as the rank and file. Tom was always held in high regard by these civil servants, who thought of him not only as a friend but also as a defender of their proper rights and prerogatives.

In any case, one of Tom's good friends was a police officer named Brian Mulhern. During the terms of several New York City mayors, Brian worked the most complicated and sometimes most threatening events in the five boroughs of New York. He served as the mayor's coordinator, mobilizing the resources of the city to solve problems with a minimum of risk and a maximum likelihood for a positive outcome. Brian was accustomed to racing off to car accidents, major fires, plane crashes, collapsed buildings, neighborhood clashes, and hostage situations. Typically, he would ride around in an unmarked Lincoln with a huge dashboard and with access to all the emergency radio channels in the New York City area. He had an amazing ability to listen to all of the channels simultaneously while still focusing on whatever required his immediate attention.

I rode with Brian on two separate occasions. On the first occasion, he picked up Tom Coleman and myself after a Notre Dame Club function in downtown Manhattan. It was about 9:30 or 10:00 at night on a spring evening. I was dressed in my clerical collar and Tom in his business suit. Our route took us quickly out of Manhattan and into the

Bronx. Brian proceeded to explore some of the more dangerous areas in that borough, pointing out where a shootout or a fire or a confrontation between police and roaming gangs had taken place. We drove not only up to the precinct that was known as Fort Apache but also down a number of dark alleys behind some of the houses. Brian took no particular notice of the young men hovering on the street corners. He simply figured that they knew that no one in his right mind would be driving in this area unless he was a policeman or with some other government agency.

The first call of the evening was a fire in one of the commercial buildings. By the time we arrived, the fire had been contained to one floor by a fairly large group of firefighters. There didn't seem to be any risk of loss of life, and everyone had been evacuated properly. No need for us to hang around. From there, we went to the scene of a car accident on one of the major thoroughfares. One or two people had already been taken away in an ambulance and, again, things seemed to be under control. Brian chatted a little with the supervisory officers on the scene.

We were near the main campus of Fordham University when a call came in about a fire at the World Trade Center. This got Brian's immediate attention, and he pulled out the red flashing light from the glove compartment, put it on the dashboard, and turned on the police siren. We made a mad dash from the Bronx down FDR Drive along the East River and then, turning along the Battery, arrived at the World Trade Center in record time.

What amazed me about that experience, especially in light of the later events of September 11, 2001, was how overwhelming it seemed. There were hundreds of firefighters and dozens of firefighting units and apparatus on the scene. There was no evident sign of fire or smoke, but as we proceeded inside one of the towers, we were informed that a fire on the third or fourth floor had been contained. As I looked up from the ground level to the top of the towers, I remember thinking, "Who in their right mind would want to go in these buildings if there was really a major fire?" It was mind-boggling to contemplate what it might require to make one's way up the stairwells to the point of emergency. Because I had my collar on and Brian had his identification, we were welcomed into the building by the firefighters and emergency workers. As became evident after September 11, a high percentage of Police and Fire Department personnel in New York City are Catholic, either in practice or in culture, and are comfortable in the presence of clergy.

We had just left the World Trade Center when a call came in about a floater, that is, an unidentified body, in the Hudson River. Brian knew that his job was not to oversee the rescue but to adjudicate the inevitable argument between the police and fire rescue units about who had responsibility for the recovery. Because of the way the two departments had evolved, especially in the face of the turmoil of the late 1960s, 1970s, and 1980s, there were occasional jurisdictional disputes between the rescue units of the Police and Fire Departments. But by the time we got to the scene, the Fire Department had recovered the body and it had been taken away. Next we got a call about a police officer in trouble. This always has the highest priority, and many cars were rushing to the scene. It turned out to be a bit of an exaggeration, but the quick presence of so many backup units solved the problem quickly.

Our final event of the evening was a call about a riot on a tour boat that was coming back to the harbor in Manhattan. We rushed to the site, which wasn't far away; it was now about one or two o'clock in the morning. We were the first unit to show up. It had begun to rain lightly. Brian got on the car radio and asked that twenty-five units be dispatched as quickly as possible. Five minutes later, fifty police officers with their billy clubs and protective gear were standing at the end of the pier ready to have the people on the boat get off single file. As it turned out, a small group of students from a local Catholic college had been in a confrontation over some romantic relationships. It was relatively easy to identify the troublemakers, and everyone else was allowed to go on their way. But as the people on the boat walked way down the file of police officers, there were Tom Coleman, Brian, and myself standing at the end of the line. I am sure that some of the student troublemakers were convinced that I was part of the administration at their school who had been quickly brought down to witness the event.

About three o'clock in the morning Brian dropped me off at my hotel. I went up thirty or forty stories and just as the door of the elevator opened on my floor, I noticed an obvious prostitute emerging from one of the rooms. She looked at me, I looked at her, she shrugged her shoulders, and I held the door of the elevator for her. Each of us having completed our work for the evening, I went to my room where I soon fell asleep. Another night in the Big City.

My second tour in the evening with Brian did not involve Tom Coleman, but rather one of our regional development directors. This time there was not quite so much action, but we did conclude the evening with a high-speed chase down FDR Drive to the scene of a major car wreck in the middle of Manhattan. I had the sense as we were halfway through our high-speed passage that our new companion was not convinced that this was a good way to spend the evening.

In many ways, New York City is safer than it was ten or fifteen years ago. Now, Brian Mulhern has retired and Tom Coleman has gone to his eternal reward. But my memories linger on about how Notre Dame provided an opportunity for me to experience firsthand some of the adrenaline-inducing excitement of a big city at night.

Active Retirement

Many of us imagine in the midst of the busyness of our lives that there will be a time in the future when we will have sufficient leisure to begin to smell the roses. Each of us may have a different dream about how we will spend this well-deserved time, time in which we will not be a prisoner of the clock, of meeting schedules, of professional and domestic responsibilities. We may see ourselves walking the lakes in a more relaxed fashion, praying at the Grotto or in the Basilica, taking on a hobby, going to more cultural and athletic events, or just sleeping in.

It is, in fact, the case that many of the staff and faculty members who retire from the university restructure their lives in ways they find productive. Many attend classes at the Forever Learning Institute. This elder-education creation of the late Father Louis Putz, C.S.C., is founded on the notion that we are never too old to learn, not just to learn in general, but to learn—keeping up on current events, mastering a new language, pursuing undeveloped talents in painting, sculpture, or knitting, or some other activity that can be shared with others. I have the good fortune to visit a Forever Learning Institute each year to talk about what's happening at Notre Dame. There are usually thirty or thirty-five people present, who listen intently and ask very good questions at the end.

Another mode of involvement is to volunteer as a tour guide or watchperson at the Basilica of the Sacred Heart or the Snite Museum or the Joyce Center. These volunteers take their responsibilities seriously and are great representatives of the university. Then there are the various groups for those who work at the university, such as ROND (Retired of Notre Dame), or the twice-yearly gatherings of retirees from the staff. Others who have made the transition into retirement are active in the University Club, where they gather for meals with their colleagues and friends, or take advantage of the more expensive dining at the Morris Inn, at least occasionally. Eating with friends on campus is a way of staying in touch and being physically drawn to Notre Dame more frequently than otherwise would be the case.

One amusing example of a happy retiree is the recently deceased Brother Ed Hagus, C.S.C., a longtime high-school teacher who settled in to semi-retirement as an in-residence person in one of the university dormitories. He had the habit of beginning the week by looking at the list of activities available to the public on campus over the next seven days and then circling those events that interested him—a play in Washington Hall or a lecture, academic or otherwise, or a concert or an athletic event. Brother Ed would eagerly await the start of the week. However, he had some kind of narcoleptic affliction that led him to fall asleep within a half-hour of sitting down. It was not unusual for Ed to show up at a lecture, often sitting near the front and fully intending to make it through to the end. But soon drowsiness would overtake him and he would fall sound asleep. He did have the good fortune of not being a snorer, so most of the people around him thought that he was just resting his eyes. When the lecture or other event was over, Ed would wake up and return to his room. His friends would tease him by asking him what the content of the lecture was. This kind of interplay went on week after week and year after year. Ed may be the best reminder that although active retirement is a worthy goal for all of us, for some of us, while the spirit is willing, the flesh is weak.

The Brevity of Fame and Fortune

On the north side of St. Joseph Lake lies Holy Cross House, the health-care and retirement facility for the Indiana Province of the Congregation of Holy Cross. About five years ago the building was renovated and expanded so that now, because of the generosity of many who supported the project with their resources, the Holy Cross community has an excellent facility with a very dedicated staff. Father André Leveille, C.S.C., the local superior, has developed a tradition of inviting Holy Cross priests from the Notre Dame community to celebrate Mass at Holy Cross House on weekdays, followed by an opportunity to join the residents for lunch. The Mass is now televised into the rooms of those medically unable to attend in person.

About a year ago I had the privilege of celebrating Mass with the Holy Cross House community with Father André concelebrating. At the beginning of Mass, Father André thanked me for coming, and I started to say the opening prayers. A few moments later I heard, from the back of the chapel, a wheelchair-bound Holy Cross brother asking the person next to him in a very loud voice, "Who is that?" His colleague replied, "Malloy." The original interlocutor came back, "What does he do?" "He's the president of Notre Dame." And with a final flourish, the questioner asked, "Whatever happened to Hesburgh?"

Thus, I was reminded of the brevity of fame and fortune. With the passage of time, men who gave their all in committed service to the university are remembered only as figures out of the past.